Mothers, Sisters, Soldiers, Spies

Mothers, Sisters, Soldiers, Spies

Women at War in American Military History

By Maureen Safford

Unbound Press

Mothers, Sisters, Soldiers, Spies: Women at War in American Military History

Series: Women Between the Lines: Overlooked Lives That Shaped History

By Maureen Safford

Copyright 2025, Unbound Press

All images remain the property of their original copyright owners. All images used are properly credited whenever possible. If any rights holder believes an image has been misused, please contact jandajtk@outlook.com to arrange proper credit or remove the image.

If images are not credited, they were created by the author using AI-assisted software. All efforts have been made to ensure originality and avoid infringement.

The publisher and author do not warrant or represent that the contents within are accurate and disclaim all warranties and are not liable for any damages whatsoever. Although all attempts were made to verify information, they do not assume responsibility for errors or omissions, and the information contained herein should not be used as a source of legal, business, accounting, financial, or any other professional advice. All content is provided 'as is.'

To the fullest extent permitted by law, the authors, contributors, and publisher disclaim liability for any loss, injury, or damages arising from the use or misuse of this book. Readers are responsible for compliance with local laws and professional standards in their jurisdiction. This edition reflects information available as of [November

2025]. Practices, regulations, and technology may change; consult current sources and institutional policies.

References to real organizations, products, devices, or services are for identification only and do not imply endorsement or affiliation. Where research findings or statistics are cited, sources are provided in notes or references. Absence of a citation does not imply universal consensus.

ISBN EBOOK 978-1-971207-07-0
ISBN Paperback 978-1-971207-09-4
ISBN Hardcover 978-1-971207-08-7

Women Between the Lines: Overlooked Lives that Shaped History:

Women Between the Lines is a nonfiction history series dedicated to recovering women's lives that have been obscured, minimized, or misrepresented in traditional historical narratives.

Across politics, war, culture, labor, and social movements, the series focuses on women whose contributions were essential but inconvenient to record—women whose work appeared in archives as footnotes, fragments, or administrative labels rather than full lives. These books do not seek to mythologize or sentimentalize. They aim to clarify: how power operated, how systems relied on women while denying them standing, and how historical memory was shaped as much by exclusion as by achievement.

The goal is not to insert women into history as an afterthought, but to reconsider history itself by examining the labor, choices, and constraints that were always present—just not centered.

Women Between the Lines is for readers who want history that is honest about complexity, attentive to structure, and willing to look directly at what was overlooked—and why.

Table of Contents

Introduction vii

Part I — War Without Permission............................. 1

Chapter 1 — Before Independence: The French and Indian War 3

Chapter 2 —The War Comes Home: The Revolutionary War 33

Part II— A Nation Divided, Women Mobilized 59

Chapter 3 — The Civil War's Unofficial Army: Nurses, Spies, and Scouts 61

Part III — The World Wars 89

Chapter 4 — World War I and the Administrative Army 91

Chapter 5 —Total War: World War II 121

Part IV — Women During Wartime in Korea, Vietnam and The Cold War: Service and Sacrifice 155

Chapter 6 — Korea and Permanent Readiness 157

Chapter 7— Vietnam: Conflict at Home and Overseas 187

Chapter 8 — Between Wars: Women and the Cold War's Turning Point 211

Part V— Modern Era: Women on the Frontlines 229

Chapter 9 — The Gulf War: Women on the Frontlines 231

Chapter 10 — Women and the War on Terror........ 251

Conclusion 269

Dedication

For the women whose work made history possible and whose names were rarely recorded.

"Those who do the work are rarely those who write the history."
— E. P. Thompson

Introduction

Why Women Have Always Been at War—Even When History Said They Weren't

America's wars have never been fought only by men. They have been fought by mothers who kept families alive when armies took the food and the labor, by sisters who ran farms and businesses when paychecks stopped, by nurses and clerks who kept men alive long enough to return to the line, and by spies and analysts who moved information faster than bullets. Some women fought in uniform. Many more fought without one because the nation needed their work, but refused to name it as service.

This book makes a simple argument: women have always been part of the American war system, and the country's success in war has repeatedly depended on women's labor. At the same time, it has repeatedly minimized or erased that contribution afterward. The pattern is not accidental. It is structural. In almost every major conflict, the same cycle repeats: crisis expands what women are permitted to do; women perform indispensable work at scale; when the crisis ends, institutions narrow the definition of "real service" again; recognition, pay, benefits, and memory lag behind reality—sometimes by generations.

That cycle shapes what you think you know about women in war. It explains why the public remembers a handful of dramatic figures—an undercover courier, a disguised soldier, a celebrated nurse—while forgetting the thousands who did the less cinematic tasks that actually make war possible: provisioning, manufacturing, paperwork, communications, transport, code work, triage, convalescence, burial details, and the rebuilding of households after the guns stop. War is not only frontlines and battles. War is a machine, and machines run on systems. Women have always been inside those systems.

This is not a book that treats women's wartime history as a string of inspirational exceptions. You will meet extraordinary individuals, because individuals give history a human face. But the core of this book is scale and structure: the jobs women did in large numbers, the constraints placed on them, and the price they paid when the nation used their service and then denied its meaning.

Across American history, women's war work has been governed by a tension between necessity and permission.

Necessity shows up when manpower collapses, casualties rise, or new forms of warfare demand new kinds of labor. Wars generate shortages—of bodies, of skills, of time—and institutions respond by pulling women closer to the center of operations. Women become nurses because the wounded do not stop arriving. Women become clerks and telephone operators because modern war runs on records and signals. Women move into factories because arsenals do not build themselves. Women enter intelligence work because information is a weapon and secrecy is a cloak that can hide discrimination as easily as it hides strategy.

Permission is what arrives with the rules: what women may do, where they may go, what they may wear, what titles they may hold, what they may be paid, what they must endure, and what they cannot report without cost.

Permission is also what arrives after war, when the country decides which kinds of labor deserve medals, pensions, or a place in memory.

Mothers, Sisters, Soldiers, Spies

This book explores the contributions of everyday women:

Mothers who keep life going when war breaks it. It includes caregiving, household survival, displacement, and the hidden logistics of food, clothing, nursing, and community stability. "Mother" here is not only biology; it is the labor of sustaining others under pressure.

Sisters are not just traditional family members, but women organizing, recruiting, fundraising, writing, transporting, connecting, persuading, recording, and remembering. "Sisterhood" can be literal family, but it also includes the social infrastructure that war requires and that institutions rarely credit.

Soldiers who were allowed formal entry into the state's machinery of war—uniformed service, regulations, discipline, rank, risk, and the politics of who gets to be called a veteran. It also includes the long history of women fighting without official recognition, and the modern struggle over combat definitions that often lag behind reality.

Spies behind information warfare: espionage, code work, translation, analysis, surveillance, and communications. In this book, spies are not a glamorous category; they are a test case for how nations build power while controlling narrative.

The blind spot this book corrects

A common misconception is that women entered war in a meaningful way only in the twentieth century and only through a handful of famous programs. Another misconception is that the story is mainly about "firsts"—the first woman to do X, the first to break Y barrier. "Firsts" matter, but they can be a trap. They create a neat progress narrative that hides two harder truths:

Women have been present throughout, often in roles treated as peripheral only because they were feminized.

Progress is not linear. Wars open doors; peace often closes them. Recognition expands; backlash follows. Institutions learn to depend on women's labor and then rebrand that labor as auxiliary again.

This book corrects that by treating women's war participation as a continuous history of work, power, constraint, and negotiation—shaped by law, culture, and the needs of the military state.

Race, class, and the uneven cost of service

No U.S. history of war and women is honest without confronting how race and class shaped who carried the heaviest burdens and who received the least credit.

For many women of color, wartime service happened inside layered systems of exclusion: segregated units, restricted assignments, barriers to training and promotion, and unequal access to benefits afterward. For Indigenous women, war often arrived not as a distant national project but as local disruption—displacement, coercion, and survival under policies made elsewhere. For immigrant and working-class women, war industries could mean wages and independence—followed by layoffs, moral policing, and pressure to return "home" once men returned from overseas. The same nation that called women essential in wartime often treated their independence as a problem in peacetime.

This book does not add women of color as a separate topic. It integrates race and class as forces that shaped the system at every stage: opportunity, assignment, exposure to risk, vulnerability to abuse, and access to recognition.

What counts as war work

A final obstacle is language. Many of the roles women held were called "support," a term that can be used to minimize. But support is not secondary; it is how war functions. A war system includes:

- sustaining troops and civilians (food, clothing, shelter, care)
- moving people and materials (transport, logistics, administration)
- sustaining the wounded and preventing disease (medicine, nursing, sanitation)
- controlling information (signals, intelligence, code work, propaganda)
- enforcing social order (policing, discipline, surveillance)
- and, of course, direct combat.

If you narrow "war work" to pulling a trigger, you will inevitably erase most women's contributions—and a large portion of men's, too. This book uses a broader, more accurate definition: war work is the labor that makes military action possible and shapes what war does to societies.

This is not a book arguing that women should be honored merely for participating. It argues that women's participation was often indispensable, and the nation's refusal to fully recognize that fact shaped policy, culture, and lives. Recognition is not symbolic. It determines pay, rank, benefits, medical care, the right to be believed, and the right to be remembered.

War reveals what a society truly values. It also shows what it is willing to hide. Women have been at war throughout American history. The question is not whether they were there. The question is: why were we taught to look past them—and what changes when we stop?

A Note on Names

In writing this book, a deliberate decision was made about how to refer to women's names. In many histories, subjects—especially military leaders—are referred to by their surnames as a sign of formality and respect. That convention remains appropriate in official records and scholarly analysis.

Here, however, women are referred to by their first names.

This decision is intentional. For much of American military history, women were treated as abstractions—categories, exceptions, auxiliaries, or "firsts"—rather than as full participants with interior lives. Using first names is one way to restore what the record often strips away: personhood.

These women were not only officers, nurses, analysts, or pioneers; they were individuals who made choices, endured consequences, and carried the weight of service in their own bodies and lives.

This choice is not meant to diminish rank, authority, or accomplishment. When rank or formality is essential to the context—particularly in discussions of command, policy, or institutional change—it is used clearly and explicitly. But where the story turns on experience, courage, or consequence, I wanted the reader to encounter these women as people first, not titles.

History has long asked women to earn recognition by conforming to its language. In this book, I ask history to bend slightly in return.

Part I — War Without Permission

Chapter 1 — Before Independence: The French and Indian War

"The calamities of war fall heaviest upon those who do not carry arms."

— William Smith Jr.

The French and Indian War and the Women Inside the War System, 1754–1763

By the time the first shots of the American Revolution echoed across Lexington Green, the women of North America had already lived through a generation of war. Not the war we remember—the one with its neat beginning in 1775, its Declaration, its Valley Forge. No, they had survived something older, messier, more intimate. A conflict that didn't announce itself with manifestos but arrived instead at kitchen doors in the middle of the night, in the crack of musket fire, in the sudden orange glow of a neighbor's burning cabin against the dark line of trees.

The struggle for independence didn't begin the story of women at war. It inherited one.

For more than a decade before "revolution" became a rallying cry, conflict had been the background noise of daily life along the frontier. Imperial rivalry. Midnight raids. Forced migrations. Alliances that could shift with a single council fire or the signing of a treaty that meant nothing to the people whose land it divided. This was the world women knew—a world where the front line wasn't a distant battlefield marked on a general's map, but your own doorway, and it could arrive without warning.

The French and Indian War—the American theater of what Europeans called the Seven Years' War—was more than a prologue to independence. It was a proving ground. A laboratory for the systems that would define the next generation of warfare. Long, fragile supply lines threaded through ancient forests and along swift rivers, connecting distant forts that guarded mountain passes, portages, and vulnerable settlements. Soldiers in bright coats and Indigenous warriors in paint fought as often in sudden ambushes as in formal, European-style battles. And information—rumor, intelligence, coded letters, whispered warnings—moved from campfires to council houses as quickly as any regiment on the march.

Civilians stood directly in the path of this violence.

Inside this world, women emerged in roles that later histories have struggled to name. They fed armies and followed them, yet were seldom counted among their ranks. They kept homesteads and entire villages alive even as those same places became targets—or refuges. Their lives became entangled with the war's most defining feature: this was a borderlands conflict where capture, adoption, displacement, and crossing between cultures weren't rare interruptions. They were part of the very structure of the fighting.

To understand this war is to see how deeply women were woven into the systems that sustained it—and how those systems, in turn, reshaped their bodies, their families, their futures.

A Clash of Cultures

Picture the backcountry of North America in the middle of the eighteenth century. A place of mounting unease. Forest paths that had carried generations of traders and Indigenous peoples now echoed with new sounds: the clatter of British packhorses, the creak of French canoes laden with trade goods and muskets.

The French and Indian War, which erupted in 1754, grew out of this crowded, contested landscape—a struggle over rivers, valleys, and forts that each side insisted were already its own. To British officials in London and colonial governors along the Atlantic seaboard, the broad Ohio River Valley represented a promise of expansion, of wealth, of empire. To French officers in Canada, it was the fragile spine connecting their settlements along the St. Lawrence to the Mississippi—a lifeline they could not afford to lose.

But long before British surveyors and French engineers inked their confident lines on maps, these same hills, forests, and waterways were homelands. The Haudenosaunee, the Shawnee, the Delaware, and dozens of other powerful Indigenous nations had their own alliances, rivalries, and memories written into the land.

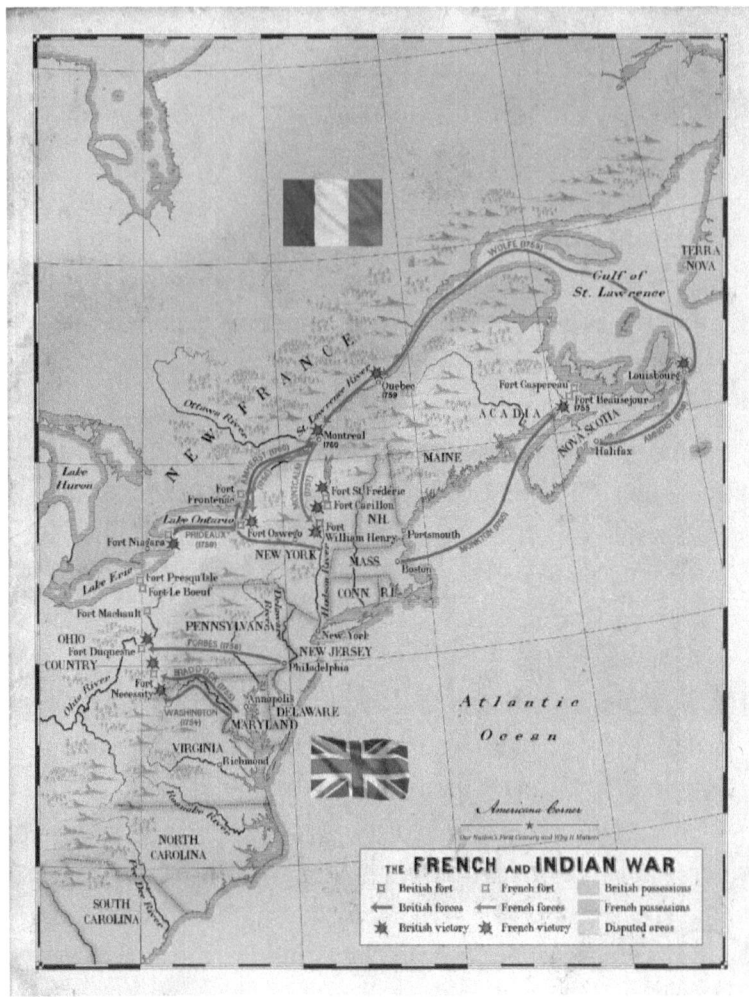

https://www.americanacorner.com/maps-colonial-era/french-and-indian-war

The name of the conflict is misleading. This was not simply "French and Indian" on one side and "British" on the other. It was a shifting, often desperate contest of empires that drew in Haudenosaunee diplomats skilled in the arts of negotiation, Shawnee and Delaware war leaders defending their territories, African and African-descended laborers whose presence is barely noted in the records, European settlers caught between competing powers, and countless people simply trying to survive.

British colonists, backed by land companies and royal charters, pressed westward from the Atlantic coast. French officers, meanwhile, constructed a chain of forts from the Great Lakes down toward the forks of the Ohio—each new log palisade a statement that their king's reach extended a little farther into the wilderness. In 1754, a young Virginia officer named George Washington led a small force into this contested terrain. His clash with French troops in the woods of what is now southwestern Pennsylvania helped ignite a war that would soon spread from the dense forests of New York to the frozen fields outside Quebec.

For men in bright uniforms, the war meant marches, sieges, formal campaigns—the stuff of military history. For families scattered along the frontier, it often meant something else entirely: waking in the night to the crack of muskets and the sudden flare of fire on the horizon. Villages emptied under threat of raids. Refugees crowded into rough stockades. News of defeats and victories traveled along the same muddy roads as pack trains and soldiers' wives.

In the camps of both French and British armies, women cooked, washed, nursed the wounded, tried to keep children alive on half rations. Their names rarely entered official reports except when they broke the rules or could no longer be ignored. Indigenous women, too, carried messages, offered counsel, endured the devastating consequences of diplomacy and warfare gone wrong—even as they helped their communities decide whether to fight, flee, or negotiate.

This war, fought from 1754 to 1763, ultimately decided that Britain—not France—would dominate most of eastern North America. But its deeper power lay in the way it unsettled lives.

In its wake came new borders, new taxes, new resentments that would help fuel another, more famous revolution. Yet many of the people who lived through these years never saw themselves as makers of grand history. They were wives following regiments up muddy roads to remote forts. Widows trying to reclaim children taken in raids. Market women trading with garrisoned soldiers. Indigenous women balancing the demands of war with the need to keep their communities fed and rooted to their homelands.

To understand the French and Indian War as women experienced it is to look beyond generals and treaties. It is to look into kitchens, encampments, missions, and stockades—into the places where the conflict pressed itself into the most intimate corners of daily life.

It is in those corners that the story of women in this war unfolds. Not as a separate tale, but as a vital part of the struggle for land, power, and survival that reshaped a continent.

Camp Followers: Allowed, Rationed, and Put to Work

Here's what the records tell us: British forces didn't simply "tolerate" women on campaign. They regulated them.

During the French and Indian War, British military practice typically permitted a limited number of women per company—often three to four—most commonly recognized in official terms as laundresses or nurses. These women could draw rations. But their presence was conditional. They were expected to work.

That arrangement exposes a theme that will run through this entire story: women were incorporated into the war effort through labor, but kept outside the status of soldiers. They were present because the war machine needed them. They were marginalized because the state preferred their work to remain "support," not service.

At places like Fort Pitt, the record becomes unusually concrete. At least ten women were associated with the Royal American Regiment at Fort Pitt in 1761—an example of practice exceeding "allowance" when necessity demanded it.

This was not decorative domesticity. Laundry mattered in an era where disease killed more soldiers than bullets ever did. Nursing mattered when medical infrastructure was fragile at best, nonexistent at worst. Cooking and clothing repair mattered when supply systems broke down—which they did, constantly. Women weren't merely traveling with the army. They were making it function.

Healers and Caretakers: Two Medical Worlds

Women's healing work in this conflict unfolded in overlapping worlds that rarely appeared together in official reports. Within British and colonial armies, in fragile frontier settlements, and across Indigenous homelands, women labored to keep people alive in conditions often designed for battle rather than survival. Their work bound these spaces together, even as the people who depended on them rarely recognized the contribution.

In British encampments and garrison towns, "nursing" was both intimate and brutally practical. It meant sitting beside shivering bodies in overcrowded huts, tending to fevers, infections, and wounds that smelled of rot and damp wool. It meant the constant, invisible labor of hauling water, washing soiled linens, scrubbing floors, managing lice and waste, trying to create some barrier between human bodies and the filth that bred disease.

Surgeons and officers might appear in the record by name. But much of the day-to-day work that made recovery possible fell to women whose presence was noted, if at all, as "wives," "camp followers," or "nurses."

Beyond the formal military system, frontier care was improvisational and relentless. In isolated cabins and small forts, women turned kitchens into sickrooms and gardens into pharmacies. They repurposed household tools for surgery and childbirth under siege conditions. They reused bandages, boiled herbs, rationed food for the wounded and the very young—often with no expectation that official help would arrive in time. If it came at all.

In these spaces, knowledge passed quietly from one woman to another. How to keep a fevered child alive through a winter night. How to move a wounded man when every sound might carry to enemy scouts. How to bury the dead when the ground was hard.

Indigenous communities, facing the same currents of war and disease, relied on their own healing networks grounded in longstanding medical and spiritual traditions. Women in many nations served as caretakers, herbalists, keepers of knowledge about plants, rituals, and communal practices that supported both bodily and spiritual balance. Their work didn't separate "medicine" from community life. Care was embedded in kinship, ceremony, reciprocal responsibility—shaping how families and villages responded to trauma, captivity, and loss.

European soldiers and settlers frequently misunderstood or dismissed these practices. Even as they sometimes sought out Indigenous remedies when their own systems failed.

The surviving records capture these medical worlds unevenly. Officers' letters, surgeons' journals, official returns mention disease, supply shortages, "female nurses"—without preserving the names or voices of the women on whom they relied. Indigenous women, in particular, often appear only in secondhand descriptions, filtered through translators, missionaries, diplomats, or enemies who didn't share their languages or priorities.

That imbalance is itself part of the story. Women's labor sustained armies, families, and communities. Yet the archive set its gaze elsewhere. To recover the medical history of this war is to learn to read around the edges of those sources—to see how much depended on people whose work was central to survival but rarely treated as central to history.

Intelligence and Information: War's Quieter Weapon

The French and Indian War relied on information in ways that feel surprisingly modern. Scouting routes. Monitoring alliances. Reading signs of attack. Judging who could be trusted. Moving messages quickly through contested terrain. Armies needed maps, guides, interpreters, and gossip as much as they needed gunpowder.

Along the shifting frontier—from forts on the Ohio to trading posts in the Great Lakes—news could mean the difference between an uneventful night and a surprise assault before dawn.

Women entered this information economy because of how daily life worked. In and around forts, they drew water, cooked, laundered clothes, tended the sick—moving between barracks, kitchens, and storehouses where soldiers and officers talked freely. In frontier towns and market spaces, they bought and sold food, cloth, and services, overhearing rumors about troop movements, supply shortages, shifting Native alliances—long before any official proclamation arrived.

Their work placed them in the current of wartime knowledge. Simply by moving through these spaces, they could observe who met in private, which traders arrived unexpectedly, when a garrison quietly doubled its night watch.

Some women acted on this information quite deliberately.

At Fort Pitt in the early 1760s, where dozens of women lived just outside the walls, movement in and out of the post was tightly regulated by passes. Commanders understood that anyone crossing that threshold could carry messages—or men—without the army's permission.

The wife of Sergeant James McIntosh, for example, was expelled from Pittsburgh after hiding deserters in her house. A minor incident, perhaps. But one that revealed how women could intervene in military discipline and communication networks simply by deciding who to shelter and who to expose.

In nearby forts and stockaded towns, officers' wives and servants often handled correspondence and relayed orders within the small world of the garrison. They became informal conduits between civilian neighbors and military command.

Indigenous women, too, moved along routes dense with information. As traders, kin, and travelers, they passed between villages and European forts, carrying not only goods but news of councils, raids, diplomatic shifts. Later accounts of Pontiac's War describe Native women warning British officers of impending attacks—or, in other cases, luring them outside the safety of walls where warriors lay in wait. Women could either stabilize or destabilize fragile alliances through what they chose to say or conceal.

Even when such stories survive only in hostile or secondhand reports, they reveal how central women were to the flow of knowledge that made diplomacy, betrayal, and survival possible in a borderlands war.

Much of this work remains half-visible in the sources. Official records describe censuses, passes, arrests, councils—but rarely pause to acknowledge the women whose errands, conversations, and decisions moved information from one world to another. Reconstructing their roles means reading those records for traces of women at the edges of the page. A wife punished for aiding deserters. A woman mentioned briefly as an interpreter's partner. A nameless "squaw" blamed for warning enemies or luring officers into ambush.

Taken together, these glimpses suggest that the war's information system wasn't just a chain of scouts and officers. It was also an intricate web of domestic tasks and social ties in which women, by necessity and sometimes by design, became makers and movers of wartime intelligence.

Captivity: The War's Most Gendered Archive

Where official reports record the sterile accounting of troop movements, rations, casualties, the stories that survive most vividly about women often come from captivity narratives.

These accounts exist because the war's violence pushed into homes, fields, and small settlements—turning domestic spaces into front lines. When raids shattered households, carrying off women and children along with men, colonial and later American audiences wanted to read about what had happened within those private worlds. As a result, women's voices—or at least versions of them—entered print in ways formal military records rarely allowed.

Yet this archive is deeply shaped by power. Captivity narratives were edited, promoted, sometimes heavily shaped by male ministers, printers, and relatives with their own religious, political, or commercial aims. They often emphasized danger, suffering, deliverance—turning a woman's experience into a moral or national lesson.

At the same time, these narratives preserve concrete details. Names. Places. Kinship ties. Everyday life within Native and colonial communities. They reveal that captivity wasn't a rare horror at the margins of the war but one of its core structures. In a borderlands conflict built on prisoner exchanges and diplomatic negotiations, captivity was a recognized—if terrifying—part of how the war worked.

The captivity of women appears even before the start of the Seven Years' War. By the beginning of the eighteenth century, New Englanders had already been telling and publishing women's captivity stories for decades.

The most well-known early example is Mary Rowlandson, captured in 1676 during King Philip's War when Native forces attacked Lancaster, Massachusetts. She spent about eleven weeks in captivity before being ransomed, and her 1682 narrative became one of the first and most influential published captivity accounts in English America.

Even before Rowlandson, colonial conflicts such as the Pequot War of 1636–1638 produced captive women and children—some forced into slavery in New England households or sold into bondage in the Caribbean. But their individual stories rarely survive in their own words.

One story, however, does survive.

It begins in Puritan colonial Maine, a generation before the French and Indian War.

The Puritan Child: Esther Wheelwright

Esther Wheelwright's life began in a world already shaped by conflict.

Born in 1696 to a Puritan family in Wells, on the Maine frontier, she grew up in a region where English settlers and Wabanaki communities lived in uneasy proximity along contested coastal lands. The boundary between these worlds was not a line on a map but a lived tension—present in every harvest season, every trading encounter, every rumor of war carried down from the north.

In 1703, during Queen Anne's War—one of the earlier imperial conflicts that set the stage for what would later be called the French and Indian War—Wabanaki raiders attacked Wells. They carried seven-year-old Esther away from her family.[1]

For her relatives, she became a symbol of loss on a dangerous frontier. A name spoken with grief. A child who might never return.

For the Wabanaki who adopted her, she became something else entirely. Kin. A child folded into a community that understood captivity and adoption not as cruelty but as part of surviving amid colonization and war. A way of replenishing families devastated by disease and violence. A way of binding former enemies into new relationships.

Raised among the Wabanaki, Esther learned a new language, new religious practices, and new patterns of daily life along the rivers and forests of what is now Maine and the Maritimes. Her early captivity was not a brief interruption—a terrifying episode before rescue and return. It was a formative childhood. One in which she moved, worked, and worshiped as a Native girl, not as a visitor awaiting deliverance.

Some years later, she was transferred into French hands and eventually arrived in Québec, where her story shifted again. Taken into the Ursuline convent school in Québec City, she entered yet another world of discipline, ritual, and female community—this time shaped by French Catholicism rather than Puritan New England or Wabanaki homelands.

In Québec, Esther did not simply pass through. She stayed.

Baptized as Marie-Esther and educated by the Ursulines, she chose to take vows as a nun and spent the rest of her life within the convent walls. In 1760, near the end of the Seven Years' War, she was elected mother superior of the Ursuline community, leading the house just as British forces captured Québec and French imperial rule collapsed.

By then, the girl taken from a Puritan settlement had become a French Catholic religious leader living in a convent, teaching young girls of French, Indigenous, and even British backgrounds.

Pause for a moment over what that means. A single woman, moving through three empires, speaking three tongues, living among three faiths—each world, in turn, laying claim to her, or lamenting her disappearance.

Her life reminds us that what we shorthand as the French and Indian War was not an isolated rupture but one episode in a long, grinding struggle for empire, a conflict whose deepest costs were often borne not on battlefields but in the lives of women pulled into war's most personal reckonings.

As a Puritan child, Wabanaki adoptee, and Ursuline nun, she embodied the layered identities that arose from raids, captivities, and cultural crossings that stretched from late seventeenth-century wars through the 1750s and 1760s.

Her life shows how wars did more than redraw maps or change flags over forts. They reordered women's languages, faiths, kinship ties, and futures—creating lives that any single empire's story could not contain.

Her story sits within, and helps illuminate, a much older pattern. One in which women's captivity was a central, recurring feature of colonial wars—not an anomaly of the French and Indian War, but a thread running through generations of conflict that shaped the continent long before independence became a dream.

The White Woman of the Genesee: Mary Jemison

The Scots-Irish Jemison family, like many immigrants of the time, had settled on the backcountry of the western frontier—what is now central Pennsylvania, in Adams County. They had cleared land, begun farming, were raising their children. Among them was twelve-year-old Mary.

At dawn in early 1755, the war came to her door. A small raiding party—six Shawnee warriors accompanied by four

Frenchmen—swept in and took Mary, her family, and a young boy from a neighboring household.

Years later, Mary would remember the deliberate efficiency of it all: the captors pausing just long enough to strip the house of bread and meat before melting back into the trees. What followed was a punishing march into the interior. The children, unable to keep pace, were whipped forward—not out of cruelty alone, but from the cold urgency of people who knew that speed was survival.

They denied them food and water, and Mary recalls that they were even forced to drink urine. They slept without shelter or fire, closely guarded by their captors through the night.[2]

At sunrise, the band stopped to share the food taken from the Jemison home. All the prisoners ate—except Mary's father, who, overcome with despair, refused. After eating, they resumed their march. As they passed Fort Canagojigge, Mary heard her father's voice for the last time.

That evening, the group stopped near a swamp to make camp again. Though they were given food, the captives found little comfort amid the fear and uncertainty they faced. A Shawnee woman gave Mary a pair of moccasins, which Mary's mother believed was a good sign that Mary might be spared. She implored Mary not to escape if given the opportunity.

That night, Mary and the young boy were led away from the others. The boy begged her to escape with him. Mary refused, recalling her mother's warnings.

That night, her worst fears were confirmed. Her parents, her siblings, and fellow captives were tomahawked, scalped, and mutilated.

After another day of walking, they camped again. That night, Mary watched them prepare the scalps of her murdered family. Each scalp was scraped, then stretched on a hoop to dry. Finally, the hair was combed and painted. Mary recognized the hair immediately. Later, the Shawnee told her they would not have killed the family if they hadn't pursued them.[3]

Mary did not know it at the time, but it was a common Seneca custom to take prisoners or scalps as part of a mourning ritual when one of their own was killed or captured in battle. The previous year, two Seneca women had lost relatives, and they were given the enemy's scalps as compensation.

It was likely that twelve-year-old Mary and the young boy were spared because they were young enough to be adopted into the tribe.

Mary was ultimately given to the two Seneca women who had lost relatives at Fort Duquesne. There was a brief ceremony near the river, and Mary was renamed Deh-hewä-nis, meaning "a pretty girl, a handsome girl, or a pleasant, good thing."

Statue of Mary Jemison, Photo by Doug Kerr from Albany, NY, United States - St. Ignatius Loyola Catholic Church

As a young woman, Mary married a Delaware man named Sheninjee, but he died shortly after their son was born. She was then taken in by his relatives and settled in Little Beard's Town, which later became present-day Cuylerville, New York. She married again, this time to a Seneca named Hiokatoo. Together, the family grew to include seven children.

She was given the opportunity to leave. She chose to remain with her adoptive community.

When Mary finally told her life story to a white interpreter, and it was published in the early nineteenth century, the resulting narrative became one of the most widely read captivity accounts in the United States.

It appealed to readers because it combined familiar elements—frontier piety, family loss, the shock of violent attack—with something more unsettling. A woman who did not simply endure captivity and then return, but who chose to remain with the people who had first taken her in.

Her narrative describes adoption rituals, agricultural work, marriage, warfare, and treaty-making. It reveals how a war that began with a raid on her childhood home eventually bound her life to Seneca lands and politics—how a girl who watched her family's scalps prepared by firelight became a Seneca woman, a mother, a keeper of memory in two worlds that could never fully reconcile.

Capture as Currency

Mary's story illustrates not a one-time rupture but a system that reordered kinship, labor, and identity. Raids brought new people into Native communities, where adoption could rebuild families shattered by earlier wars and epidemics. Captives, especially women and children, carried languages, skills, and memories across cultural boundaries, reshaping both the communities they joined and those they left behind. For colonists, their absence fueled petitions, military campaigns, and later efforts to "recover" or "rescue" those who had been taken; for Indigenous nations, their presence became part of strategies for survival in a landscape transformed by imperial rivalry.

Many women were captured, some returned to families that no longer recognized them, and others, like Jemison, refused to leave the communities that they now belonged to.

The Missing Voices

Enslaved African and African-descended women experienced the French and Indian War as yet another layer of captivity in lives already defined by coercion. Bound within systems in which others legally owned their labor, movement, and bodies, they moved through a landscape shaken by raids, marches, and forced relocations they neither chose nor could escape.

Laws in French and British colonies made enslavement hereditary through the mother, so women's reproductive lives were treated as part of the machinery of empire: children born to enslaved women were automatically enslaved, ensuring that war, displacement, and plantation economics rested on their capacity to bear and raise future laborers.

The record shows that enslaved women were sold away from their families, marched with troops or supply parties, and subjected to sexual violence with little legal recourse, even as officials debated how to regulate interracial relationships for the "good" of the colony.

Specific lives occasionally surface through this uneven archive. In French Canada, enslaved women such as Marie-Joseph Angélique appear in legal records because of moments of crisis.

Marie-Josèphe dite Angélique (ca. 1705-1734) was a Madeira-born black enslaved woman who lived in New France in the early 1700s and was executed for setting fire to her enslaver's home in Montreal in 1734.[4] Other enslaved women appear as property in wills, court cases, or parish registers in New France and Louisiana, their pregnancies, sales, and deaths tracked for financial rather than human reasons.

These scattered traces underline how captivity worked in gendered ways: women's bodies, sexual exploitation, and their roles as mothers and kin-makers placed them at the center of how colonial societies replenished themselves, even when the official narrative insisted the real action lay with armies and generals.

Indigenous women's lives were likewise not adjacent to conflict; they were entangled with it at every level.

The French and Indian War and its related campaigns brought raids and reprisals that deliberately targeted women and children—British and colonial leaders openly discussed capturing Native families to force warriors to "tremble" for their loved ones and to break the power of resistant communities. Warfare meant the destruction of crops and orchards, primarily cultivated by women, the burning of villages, hunger, and the forced movement of whole communities into new territories or closer to colonial centers.

Alliance politics added further pressure to women's lives: marriages between Indigenous women and French or British traders, for example, cemented commercial and diplomatic ties in the Ohio and Mississippi valleys, turning women and their children into living bridges between competing worlds.

Yet the historical record rarely names Indigenous women as actors, even when their presence is evident between the lines. Missionaries, officers, and colonial officials acknowledged that French traders married Native women to secure access to furs and safe passage. Still, those women usually appear only as "wives" or "squaws," without personal names or voices.

Studies of colonial traffic in Native women have shown that women were captured, traded, or enslaved, especially in French and Spanish spheres, where Indigenous captives—disproportionately women and children—could be absorbed into households as both laborers and kin, their identities reshaped by violence.[5]

New France and "Panis" captives

In New France (Canada), Indigenous captives from the interior were legally and socially lumped under the label "Panis," a catch-all term for many Native groups whose members were taken in war and sold into slavery. Parish registers and notarial records in Quebec and Montreal document Indigenous women and girls identified as "Panis" in baptism, sale, or inheritance documents, often marked as domestic slaves in French households.

These women labored in homes as maids, laundresses, and childcare providers; some were also coerced into sexual relationships, producing mixed-descent children whose status was negotiated within the household.

Traffic in Native Women

In the lower Mississippi Valley and Gulf Coast, French and later Spanish colonists purchased or seized Indigenous women—Natchez, Chitimacha, Chaouacha, and other nations—and used them as domestic servants, field laborers, and concubines.

A 1706 French royal order, for example, authorized the enslavement of the Chitimacha following conflict in Louisiana. Subsequent records show Chitimacha women and children held as slaves in colonists' households—their names, if recorded at all, appearing in estate inventories alongside furniture and livestock.

Studies of the Mississippi Valley document Indigenous and African enslaved women sharing space in colonial homes—working side by side in kitchens, fields, and nurseries. Native women's roles could blur between coerced labor and quasi-kinship as they bore children to European men. These relationships were rarely marriages in any legal sense, yet they created ties that colonists exploited for political advantage and personal profit.

Scholarship on colonial traffic in Native American women highlights how women were captured in intertribal wars, then sold or gifted to French or Spanish authorities—or redistributed among allied Indigenous groups, often to cement political ties. This was not random violence. It was systematic. Strategic.

Because women and children were more easily incorporated into households than adult men, they were disproportionately targeted. As domestic workers. As potential wives or concubines. As a means to replace losses from disease and warfare that had devastated both Indigenous and colonial populations.

The archive preserves these transactions in ledgers, letters, and legal disputes—but rarely in the voices of the women themselves. What remains are the structures that bound them: the laws that authorized their enslavement, the households that claimed their labor, the children born into ambiguous status between nations and empires. Wars shaped their lives; they did not start in a region where captivity and enslavement were woven into the very fabric of colonial expansion.

Identities Reshaped by Violence

In these systems, Indigenous women's original names, languages, and family ties were often erased or altered in the records; baptismal entries replaced Native names with Christian ones, and notarial acts described them primarily by status ("Panis slave," "Indian girl") rather than by origin or kinship.

Over time, some women and their children were folded into colonial society as "domestics," "servants," or recognized partners of European men. Still, that incorporation rested on initial acts of capture, sale, and coerced relocation.

Taken together, these stories reveal a pattern: Indigenous women stood at the crossroads of diplomacy, economy, and survival, but the documents that survive were crafted to measure land, tribute, and allegiance, not to honor women's decisions, grief, or endurance.

[1] Ann M. Little, The Many Captivities of Esther Wheelwright (New Haven: Yale University Press, 2016), 1–3

[2] James E. Seaver, A Narrative of the Life of Mrs. Mary Jemison (1824; repr., New York: American Scenic and Historic Preservation Society, 1907), 25–27

[3] James E. Seaver, A Narrative of the Life of Mrs. Mary Jemison (1824; repr., New York: American Scenic and Historic Preservation Society, 1907), 31.

[4] Afua Cooper, The Hanging of Angélique: The Untold Story of Canadian Slavery and the Burning of Old Montréal (Toronto: HarperCollins, 2006)

[5] See, for example, Juliana Barr, "Colonial Traffic in Native American Women," Journal of American History 96, no. 1 (2009); Dana Velasco Murillo, "Indigenous Women in New Spain's Silver Mining District, Zacatecas, Mexico, 1620–1770," Hispanic American Historical Review 93, no. 2 (2013)

Chapter 2 —The War Comes Home: The Revolutionary War

"Remember the Ladies."

— Abigail Adams

Beyond the Battlefield

The American Revolution did not introduce women to war. It reorganized a system they already knew.

For decades before independence, women in colonial North America had lived inside recurring imperial conflicts—supplying armies, nursing the sick, surviving raids, navigating captivity, and absorbing the consequences of violence that rarely stopped at battle lines. When rebellion turned into war, those same structures expanded. Women were already there.

What changed was scale. What did not change was status.

Following the Army—Again.

When the Continental Army moved, it rarely moved alone. Behind the columns of men marched a shadow population of wives, sisters, daughters, servants, and enslaved women, who cooked, washed, nursed, scavenged, traded, carried, and buried. Women worked as "sutlers," selling goods to soldiers when official supply lines failed. What they received for this was limited and precarious. In some camps, "dependent" women were issued a daily ration, but unless formally employed by the army (as laundresses, nurses, cooks), they generally did not receive wages

Later generations would describe the Revolution as a contest of ideals and battlefield maneuvers. But for those who lived it, war was also hunger, exposure, disease, and the hard math of whether an army could stay alive long enough to fight. In that daily struggle, women were not a footnote. They were part of the mechanism that kept soldiers functioning.

Commanders often described these women as a burden. In practice, they were a necessity. Clean clothing reduced disease. Cooked food sustained morale. Nursing kept men alive long enough to fight again. The Continental Army's logistical weakness made women's work even more critical than it had been under British imperial command. Once again, the contradiction was clear: women's labor was essential to military survival, but their wartime labor was not fully recognized as service. Even when the army depended on women's work, it often framed those women as dependents—mouths to feed—rather than workers performing tasks the army itself could not or would not staff.

Women of Color in a War of Liberty

For women of color, the Revolution sharpened longstanding contradictions rather than resolving them.

Enslaved and free Black women navigated a world in which "liberty" was a rallying cry, a promise, and a trap. Their daily work kept armies and households functioning, yet their names, choices, and risks rarely appeared in the new nation's self-narrative.

Enslaved Women: Danger and Possibility

For enslaved women, war meant sudden movement. And sometimes, opportunity. They were forced to travel with Patriot or Loyalist owners when armies shifted—driving wagons, cooking, caring for children on the march. Their labor kept households functioning even as those households fled from one contested region to another, following the fortunes of war.

But others seized the confusion of war to run.

They slipped away to British lines or Continental camps, hoping one side's desperation would open a path to freedom. It was a calculated gamble—a choice made in the dark, with incomplete information and enormous risk.

Lord Dunmore's 1775 proclamation in Virginia, promising freedom to the enslaved who joined British forces, drew not only men but also women and children to his ships and encampments.[1] Women who could not serve as soldiers labored as laundresses, cooks, and nurses—risking re-enslavement or violent punishment if captured. They performed the same roles they had always performed, but now under a different flag, with the fragile promise of freedom attached.

These choices rarely brought safety.

Disease tore through crowded British refugee camps and ships. Smallpox. Typhus. Dysentery. The very places that promised liberation became death traps. Patriot forces who retook runaways often sold them south—deeper into slavery, farther from any hope of return—or punished them as traitors to the cause of American liberty.

Some enslaved women attached themselves to the Continental Army instead, hoping that service might persuade white officers or legislatures to grant them freedom afterward. It was a different bet on the same desperate hope: that loyalty, labor, and sacrifice might be rewarded with the freedom revolutionary rhetoric promised to everyone else.

Runaway ads from the period describe women who had "gone to camp"—a phrase that suggests both flight and destination. Joining the army's moving world—as servants, laundresses, or cooks—could be both an act of survival and a declaration. A refusal to wait passively for liberty to be handed to them. These women understood something the architects of revolution preferred not to acknowledge: that the war for independence was also a war over who would be free and on whose terms. They made their choices in that knowledge, navigating between armies that both needed their labor and denied their humanity—seeking freedom in a conflict that would leave most of them still enslaved when the fighting finally stopped.

Washington's Women at Valley Forge

Free Black women performed much of the same work as white camp followers, but with fewer protections and almost no access to the pensions or public honors that later trickled to some white veterans' families. In Continental encampments, they washed uniforms, nursed the sick, cooked, and sometimes traveled long distances alongside regiments, receiving rations but often little or no pay.

Hannah Archer Till and Margaret Thomas

At Valley Forge, for example, two women, Margaret Thomas, a free Black woman, and Hannah Till, an enslaved woman hired out to Washington, worked as a laundress and seamstress attached to George Washington's staff, sharing responsibilities.[2]

Hannah Archer Till's life spanned the war's full geography. From the eastern shores, where she was born enslaved, to becoming a free Black matriarch admired by the general she had served. Born around 1721 in Kent County, Delaware, she entered the world already marked by overlapping identities and power structures: her father was Oneida, her mother an African-descended enslaved woman, and her first name, Long Point, commemorated her father's successful hunt for a buck.

As a teenager, she was sold from her first owner and sent to Pennsylvania, beginning a pattern of forced movement that would continue for decades. By twenty-five, she had been sold again, this time taken across the Atlantic to Northumberland, England, before she was brought back and purchased by Reverend John Mason of the Associate Reformed Church in New York. Each sale severed local ties and imposed new ones, yet she carried her skills—and eventually her family—through every upheaval.

On the eve of the American Revolution, Hannah married Isaac Till, an enslaved man in Bergen County, New Jersey. Around 1777, George Washington leased both Hannah and Isaac to work as cooks, with their names appearing in his wartime expense book as part of the moving household that sustained his campaigns.[3]

The couple already had three children when the army marched into winter quarters at Valley Forge in 1777–1778. There, in the cramped Isaac Potts house that served as Washington's headquarters, Hannah cooked for the general's table while the army shivered and sickened around them.[4] In the middle of that brutal winter, she gave birth to a fourth child, Isaac Worley Till, around January 1778.

Hannah's war did not end with Valley Forge.

For six and a half years, she accompanied Washington on campaign, her work following him from encampment to encampment as armies shifted across the colonies. For six months, she also served in the household of the Marquis de Lafayette, which meant that between her two employers, she was present at every battle in which Washington or Lafayette participated during the war.

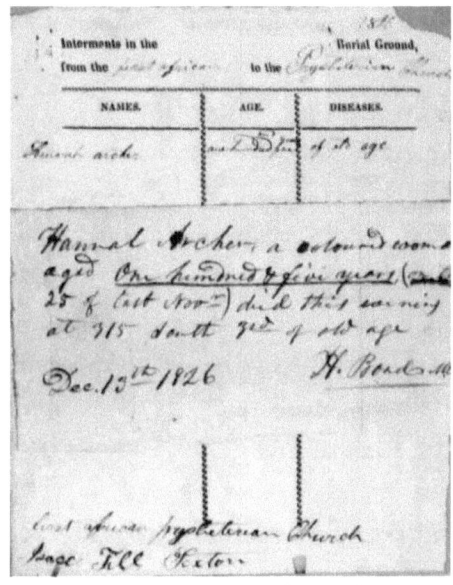
Muster Roll of Hannah Archer, Valley Forge

In 1778, after years of unpaid and underpaid labor, Hannah and Isaac managed an extraordinary act: they purchased their freedom, a transaction recorded as taking place on October 30 or in December of that year, depending on the source. Even afterwards, Hannah worked as a paid cook for Washington, shifting her status within the same war system—from leased property in his service to a free wage-earning woman whose skills he continued to rely on.

After the Revolution, the Tills moved to Philadelphia, a city that had become both a political capital and a center of

Black religious life. There they joined the First African Presbyterian Church, anchoring their large family, which eventually included seven children, in a free Black community that blended spiritual support with mutual aid. Hannah continued to cook for a living, her work sustaining her household long after armies disbanded.

Decades later, when Lafayette returned to the United States on his celebrated 1824–1825 tour, he sought out "Aunt Hannah" in Philadelphia, learned that the elderly woman who had once cooked for him was behind on her mortgage, and quietly paid it off. That same year, Hannah, then about 102 years old, was interviewed for the Annals of Philadelphia, preserving a rare glimpse of an enslaved-born woman whose memories stretched from colonial Delaware to the Age of Revolution.

Hannah Archer Till died in 1826 at roughly 104, having lived long enough to see the new nation stabilize but not to see slavery end.

Her body, like her life, did not rest in one place: first buried in the graveyard of First African Presbyterian Church in Philadelphia, her remains were later moved when that cemetery was sold, first to Lebanon Cemetery and eventually to Eden Cemetery in Collingdale, Pennsylvania. In 2015, nearly two centuries after her death, the Daughters of the American Revolution formally honored her as a Patriot at Eden Cemetery, recognizing that the Revolution's story of endurance, logistics, and sacrifice runs through women like Hannah whose names once appeared only in ledgers and footnotes.

Her life makes visible a world in which an enslaved woman could feed generals, bear children in war headquarters, buy her own freedom, and die as a free Black elder remembered by the men and communities she had quietly sustained.

Women in the Margins

The Revolution did not resolve the contradictions in women of color's lives; it magnified them. Enslaved women could carry messages, mend uniforms, nurse wounded men who spoke of freedom, and still see children sold or futures constrained by laws that treated them as property. Free Black women might share tents, tasks, and dangers with white camp followers while knowing that the new republic offered them no clear place in its political community.

Their experiences reveal a war in which women of color stood at the heart of logistical and emotional survival, even as the language of liberty moved past them toward a narrower vision of whose freedom counted.

Survival, Resistance, and Indigenous Women in the Revolution

The record of this era, written mainly by colonial and later American observers, rarely names Indigenous women directly. Yet their presence is evident in the consequences: who survived, who relocated, who rebuilt.

The Revolution was not only a colonial rebellion against Britain. It was also a war that tore through Indigenous homelands, alliances, and survival systems. Some Native nations and communities aligned with the American cause, others with the British, and many were pulled into conflict by geography and coercion rather than choice.

Indigenous women faced the Revolution as a continuation of imperial warfare fought on their homelands. Alliance decisions made by male leaders had immediate consequences for women: lost villages, disrupted communities, forced migration, and the responsibility of sustaining families amid devastation.

One documented example involves the Oneida, who supported American forces during critical periods. Sources describe the story of Polly Cooper, an Oneida woman remembered for walking hundreds of miles to aid George Washington's starving army during the winter at Valley Forge.[5]

Traveling with a small delegation of roughly forty to fifty Oneida (and some Seneca) men, she helped carry bushels of white corn from central New York to Pennsylvania, a journey of about 250–400 miles through cold, snow, and deep mud. The corn alone was not enough; crucially, Polly taught the soldiers how to hull and cook it properly, turning it into nourishing soup often mixed with nuts or fruit. Eaten raw or improperly prepared, the grain could make them ill rather than save their lives.

Polly remained in the encampment after some of the Oneida warriors returned home, tending sick soldiers, sharing knowledge of medicinal and wild foods, and, in some traditions, serving as a cook in Washington's military household.[6]

She refused payment for her work, and later accounts report that Martha Washington and officers' wives presented her with a black shawl in gratitude. That gift is preserved by Oneida descendants as a symbol of alliance and reciprocity. Today, Polly Cooper is honored in Oneida oral tradition, regional historical societies, and museum exhibits as an icon of Oneida support for the Patriot cause and as a woman whose labor and expertise quietly sustained the Continental Army through one of its darkest winters.

Whether told as a specific individual narrative or as an emblem of Oneida aid more broadly, the point is structural: an army on the edge of starvation could not live on ideology. It lived on food.

This is another pattern that will repeat in later wars: women's contributions are often most visible at the moment of crisis—when survival hangs by a thread—and are most easily minimized after the crisis passes.

Statue of Polly Cooper

Madam Sacho

Another glimpse of Indigenous women's experience during the Revolutionary War comes not from triumph, but from survival.

Madam Sacho enters the written record as her world is coming apart. In the late summer of 1779, General John Sullivan led a large American army into Haudenosaunee country—lands of the Six Nations of the Iroquois Confederacy—under orders from George Washington to break the power of those nations that had sided with or were assumed to support the British.

Sullivan's troops burned villages, cut down orchards, and destroyed fields of corn, beans, and squash, the core of Haudenosaunee subsistence and the product of generations of women's labor. In this scorched landscape, American officers came upon an elderly woman left behind in an empty village.

The soldiers called her many things: "a very old Squaw," "helpless, impotent wretch," and "antediluvian hag." Only one recorded a name: "Madam Sacho."

She was alone, sick, and nearly blind in an abandoned house in an Oneida settlement along the army's route, surrounded by the wreckage of a community that had fled before the advancing troops. She told them that her family and neighbors had gone, leaving her because she was too old and infirm to travel quickly over rough country under the threat of attack.

American accounts describe her as dignified and composed despite weakness and hunger, a woman who had lived her entire life rooted in the village and fields that now lay in ashes around her. Officers recorded that she spoke of the corn that had been destroyed and the coming winter, bearing witness in a few sentences to the wider catastrophe that Sullivan's men were inflicting on Haudenosaunee communities.

Some of the soldiers, moved by her plight, debated what to do. The campaign's purpose was to drive the Haudenosaunee from their homelands by destroying food stores and settlements, not to care for those left behind. Yet officers ultimately ordered that Madam Sacho be given food and clothing and transported with the army for at least part of its march, a gesture recorded in journals as proof of their humanity even as they continued to burn other towns and fields.

Her presence in these records, while filtered through the eyes and language of American officers, highlights the gendered impact of the campaign: an elderly woman, anchored to place by age and disability, made visible to history only because invading soldiers chose to write about the moment they encountered her.

What is known of Madam Sacho's fate after the campaign is fragmentary. Accounts suggest she was eventually left in the care of missionaries or at a frontier settlement, dependent on strangers for survival.

There is no surviving narrative in her own voice, no record of how she understood the loss of her village or the forced migration of her kin into British territory or farther west. Yet brief references to her in Revolutionary War journals capture the broader reality of the Sullivan Campaign for Haudenosaunee women: war as the destruction of crops they had planted, houses they had maintained, and communities they had held together, leaving the elderly and the vulnerable stranded in a suddenly hostile landscape.

Madam Sacho stands in the record as both an individual and a symbol of how the Revolution's frontier warfare fell with particular force on Native women. She represents a category of women whose heroism lay in enduring and surviving systematic annihilation. Her story is not preserved because she held rank or wielded formal authority.

It survives because scorched-earth warfare left devastation so complete that even enemy observers recorded it. While Indigenous women were not peripheral to the Revolution, they were among those who paid its highest costs.

Information as a Weapon

The Revolution depended on information as much as force. Intelligence work was informal, decentralized, and often invisible by design. Women participated not because they were granted authority, but because their daily lives placed them inside networks of movement, conversation, and trust.

Women served as messengers, observers, and intermediaries—sometimes intentionally, sometimes because their labor brought them into spaces where information circulated freely. The same assumptions that framed women as non-threatening could make them effective conveyors of knowledge.

While the archival record for Revolutionary espionage is uneven, the structural point is sound: irregular war produces irregular intelligence, and women were positioned inside it.

Agent 355: The Phantom Spy of the Culper Ring

Espionage in the Revolutionary era is often romanticized, but at its core, it was logistics and information: who moved where, what supplies were scarce, who could be trusted, which roads were passable, and which loyalties were shifting. Women were well-positioned for this work precisely because their movements could appear unthreatening, or because their work placed them in spaces where men spoke freely.

Agent 355 exists at the edge of the archival record, where verifiable intelligence work meets later legend. What is known for certain is that "355" appears in the numerical codebook used by Major Benjamin Tallmadge's Culper spy network—and that the number 355 simply meant "lady."

In a 1779 letter, Abraham Woodhull (code name Samuel Culper Sr.) wrote that he planned to go into New York and, "by the assistance of a 355 of my acquaintance, shall be able to outwit them all," a line that confirms the existence of at least one woman whose help he considered crucial to his work. From that single documented reference, later writers have built the figure remembered as Agent 355: a female informant operating in Loyalist and British social circles, capable of eliciting information that male officers would never share openly with a known rebel sympathizer."[7]

Within that narrow evidentiary frame, historians agree on a few core points and debate many others. The Culper Ring did, in fact, provide George Washington with detailed intelligence on British troop dispositions, shipping, and plans, especially in New York City. The sudden improvement in the quality of army-level information after Woodhull's mention of "a 355" suggests that a woman (or women) with access to high-ranking Loyalists and British officers began feeding the network insights from elite drawing rooms, offices, and gatherings.

Some later accounts credit Agent 355 with helping uncover Benedict Arnold's treason and contributing to the capture of British spymaster Major John André, who was seized with incriminating plans for West Point concealed in his boot. However, those specific attributions rest on inference rather than direct documentary proof.

Speculation about her identity ranges widely. Candidates have included Anna Strong of Setauket, whose clothesline signals helped coordinate Culper communications on Long Island; Mary or Sally Townsend of a prominent Loyalist-leaning family in New York; and an unnamed woman from a well-connected Tory household, moving easily in André's social orbit and perhaps close to Arnold as well.

Some researchers argue that "Agent 355" was never a single figure at all, but a convenient code category for any woman whose information Woodhull and his associates used, meaning that several women's work may have been collapsed into one shadowy persona over time.

What remains historically sound is this: the Culper Ring relied on women as observers and go-betweens in British-held New York, and at least one of those women was important enough for Woodhull to single out as someone who could "outwit them all," even though her name—and the precise extent of her achievements—never made it into the surviving record.

Fighting Without Permission

As in earlier wars, a small number of women entered direct combat roles by disguising themselves as men. The most documented case remains Deborah Sampson, who served in the Continental Army under a male name for roughly seventeen months. Sampson's military service matters, but what followed matters more.

Deborah Sampson: The Soldier Who Defied Convention

When Deborah Sampson bound her chest with linen strips and cut her hair short in 1782, she transformed herself into Robert Shurtliff, a young Continental Army recruit ready to fight for American independence. Her decision to disguise herself as a man was not merely an act of personal courage—it was a calculated response to a society that denied women the right to serve their country openly, even as the nation fought for the very principles of liberty and equality.

Deborah Sampson's story begins in hardship long before she ever put on a uniform. Born in 1760 in Massachusetts, she grew up in a poor family, was bound out as an indentured servant, and learned to work alongside men in the fields, acquiring physical strength and practical skills that would later serve her in war. By the time she reached her early twenties, the Revolution had been raging for years, yet formal military service remained closed to women; they could nurse, cook, or follow the army as dependents, but not take up arms as soldiers.

In 1782, as the war dragged on and manpower thinned, Deborah made a radical decision: she bound her chest, donned men's clothing, and enlisted under the name Robert Shurtliff in the Massachusetts Line of the Continental Army. Eighteenth- and nineteenth-century armies were porous institutions. Recruitment was rushed, recordkeeping uneven, and medical examinations rudimentary. Many male soldiers were young, slight, illiterate, or physically impaired. In that environment, sex could be concealed—especially when uniforms, short hair, shared hardship, and distance from home flattened differences.

Disguise worked not because armies were progressive, but because armies were desperate. As long as a soldier performed adequately, officers often preferred not to look too closely. This pragmatic tolerance tells us something essential: combat effectiveness routinely mattered more than gender—until gender became visible.

Against this backdrop, Deborah's act was both deeply personal and profoundly political—a way of claiming a place in a struggle whose rhetoric of liberty had not yet included women.

As "Robert," she joined a light infantry company used for scouting, raiding, and rapid maneuvers. She participated in skirmishes in New York's lower Hudson Valley, including actions near Tarrytown and perhaps along the paths connecting British posts and Loyalist farms, enduring the same long marches, poor rations, and exposure as her comrades. In one engagement, she received a sword cut to the head and, more dangerously, a musket ball in the thigh; desperate to prevent army surgeons from discovering her sex, she reportedly removed the bullet herself with a sewing needle and her knife, tending the wound in secret.

For months, she maintained her disguise, sharing tents, guard duty, and battle lines with other soldiers who knew her only as a quiet, competent young man. That daily performance—washing, dressing, speaking, and moving in ways that would arouse no suspicion—was itself a form of constant, embodied risk layered over the dangers of combat.

Her hidden identity finally unraveled not in battle but in illness. In 1783, she fell seriously ill in Philadelphia and was taken to a hospital. There, Dr. Barnabas Binney discovered that "Robert" was a woman. Instead of immediately exposing her to public disgrace, he quietly removed her from the hospital and informed General George Washington through private channels. Washington, facing the complex politics of a war almost won and an army on the verge of disbanding, arranged for her to receive an honorable discharge rather than a court-martial or public humiliation.[8]

She left the army in October 1783, with papers that preserved her reputation as a good soldier without explicitly revealing her secret. Deborah then petitioned the Massachusetts State Legislature for pay the army had withheld because of her gender. Her petition was granted, and she was awarded a pension of 34 pounds plus interest, backdated to her 1783 discharge.

Additionally, in 1816, Congress approved a pension request (the only one for a woman), and she received a monthly payment from the Massachusetts Invalid Pension Roll.[9] The pension fight is not a sidebar. It is an early expression of the long war over recognition. Women could be essential during conflict and still be treated as anomalous afterward—exceptions to be judged, debated, and, often, reluctantly compensated.

Deborah Sampson married Benjamin Gannett of Sharon, Massachusetts, became a farmer's wife, and struggled with the lingering effects of her wartime injuries and poverty. To supplement her income, she traveled and gave lectures about her experiences, sometimes appearing on stage in a soldier's uniform and demonstrating drill, then changing into a dress to underscore the contrast between gendered expectations and what she had done.

Her life—poor farm girl, self-fashioned soldier, pensioned veteran, and public storyteller—exposed the gap between revolutionary ideals and women's legal status. By stepping into a role the new nation insisted she could not hold, Deborah Sampson forced Americans to confront the reality that courage, endurance, and patriotism were not confined to men, even if the laws and institutions of the era did their best to pretend otherwise.

Deborah "Robert" Sampson

But Deborah wasn't alone. Her story stands out because documentation survives. Many others are known only through fragments: court-martial records, newspaper anecdotes, pension affidavits, or later recollections of uneven reliability. The unevenness is not accidental. Women discovered in uniform were often quietly discharged, returned home, or absorbed back into civilian life without ceremony. There was no institutional incentive to preserve their stories.

Some cases surface because the discovery created a scandal. Others appear because disability or poverty forced women to petition for aid. In both instances, the archive privileges conflict over continuity. What disappears are the women who served, were never discovered, and left no trace because the system had no place to record them.

What is striking is how rarely discovery led to institutional reflection. The presence of capable women in the ranks did not produce policy reconsideration. Instead, it produced reaffirmation of the boundary. The problem, in official eyes, was not that women had fought, but that they had done so without authorization.

Later retellings often celebrate these women as extraordinary—stronger, braver, more determined than others. That framing flatters, but it misleads. These women were not anomalies in ability. They were anomalies in access. Calling them exceptions allows institutions to preserve the rule. It suggests that gender exclusion failed only rarely, rather than functioning exactly as designed. By focusing on disguise, we risk missing the larger point: women fought not because the system welcomed them, but because war made the system temporarily permeable.

The Postwar Reckoning Begins Early

When independence was secured, women faced a familiar reckoning. Their labor had been required. Their recognition was optional.

For many women, the Revolution's aftermath meant economic instability, widowhood, disability, and the bureaucratic struggle to translate sacrifice into support. Pension systems were limited, inconsistent, and often shaped around male military norms. Women frequently entered the record not because institutions tracked their service, but because women fought for assistance.

They had carried the war on their backs; now they carried its aftermath through courts, legislatures, and the slow grind of recognition. Widows petitioned for support. Nurses sought acknowledgment. Women who had followed armies returned to precarious civilian lives. The structures for recognition were narrow, gendered, and inconsistent. The Revolution promised citizenship while leaving most women outside its formal boundaries.

The war had expanded women's roles. Peace narrowed them again.

Legacy and Impact: How Revolutionary Women Shaped Future Generations

The Revolutionary War did not create gender equality. But it did develop precedents that mattered:

- It normalized women's presence in wartime systems—camp labor, nursing, provisioning, communications, intelligence networks—without fully legitimizing those roles.
- It generated a documentary trail of women demanding recognition through petitions and

pensions—early proof that women understood their work as service even when the state did not.
- It revealed how war could temporarily expand women's roles, only for postwar culture to narrow them again.

The pattern begins here. The United States asked women for wartime labor long before it offered women full citizenship. It depended on women long before it thanked them. And it built much of its early military endurance on work it preferred not to name.

[1] John Murray, Earl of Dunmore, "Lord Dunmore's Proclamation," Virginia Gazette (Williamsburg), November 14, 1775; see also Sylvia R. Frey, Water from the Rock: Black Resistance in a Revolutionary Age (Princeton, NJ: Princeton University Press, 1991), 69–72.
[2] "The Women Present at Valley Forge," National Park Service, Valley Forge National Historical Park; "Running from Bondage," Museum of the American Revolution.
[3] "Hannah Till," U.S. National Park Service; "Hannah Till (ca. 1718–1826) & Isaac Till," Morris-Jumel Mansion.
[4] "Hannah Till," U.S. National Park Service; Washington's Headquarters, Valley Forge National Historical Park (brochure).
[5] "Polly Cooper," Valley Forge Muster Roll; "The Polly Cooper Shawl: Testimony to a Pact of the Revolutionary War," Oneida Indian Nation; "Polly Cooper," American Battlefield Trust.
[6] Karim M. Tiro, "Madam Sacho: How One Iroquois Woman Survived the American Revolution," Humanities 36, no. 3 (2015).
[7] Benjamin Tallmadge, "Culper Code Book," ca. 1779, George Washington Papers, Library of Congress.
[8] See Deborah Sampson's service record summarized in Massachusetts Soldiers and Sailors of the Revolutionary War, vol. 14, 164, and "Deborah Sampson," National Women's History Museum
[9] See "Deborah Sampson," National Women's History Museum, and "Deborah Sampson," George Washington's Mount Vernon digital encyclopedia

Part II— A Nation Divided, Women Mobilized

Chapter 3 — The Civil War's Unofficial Army: Nurses, Spies, and Scouts

"The war had entered our houses."

— Mary Chesnut

THE AMERICAN CIVIL WAR (1861–1865) was fought over the preservation of the Union and the future of slavery in the United States, in a republic that had argued over both since its founding.

What began as a constitutional and political crisis—eleven Southern states seceding after the election of a Republican president—became a test of whether a nation built on both freedom and human bondage could continue in the same form. The war forced questions that compromise had postponed: who counted as a citizen, what the Union meant, and whether enslaved people would remain property or become people in law as they had always been in fact.

Armies of unprecedented size marched and fought from the Atlantic coast to the Mississippi River and beyond, turning farms, crossroads, and small towns into battlefields. Railroads, factories, and telegraph lines wove the conflict together, making it the first American war fought with truly industrial means.

Rifled muskets, artillery, and entrenchments produced slaughter on a scale that stunned contemporaries, while blockades, scorched-earth campaigns, and military occupation brought the war into kitchens, fields, and churchyards. The line between battlefront and home front frayed as civilians endured destruction, hunger, flight, and the constant uncertainty of living in a landscape that could turn hostile overnight.

By 1865, Union victory had shattered the Confederacy, destroyed slavery in law, and vastly expanded the reach of the federal state. The Thirteenth Amendment ended slavery, but emancipation opened as many questions as it answered: how freedom would be lived, who would enforce it, and whether the nation that emerged from the war would honor the claims of formerly enslaved people to land, security, and political voice.

More than 600,000 soldiers had died, and countless civilians had been displaced or impoverished. The social and political aftershocks of the conflict would shape American life for generations, as Reconstruction and its unmaking carried the war's unfinished arguments into the decades that followed.

Nurses, Spies, Scouts, and Survivors

Once again, wartime expanded women's roles. This time, however, it industrialized them. The scale of killing forced the United States—especially the Union—to build systems of care, supply, and information to match the scale of modern war.

Those systems were not built by generals alone. They were built in hospitals, rail depots, relief societies, contraband camps, and clandestine networks—places where women worked in numbers too large to dismiss as anecdote.

And yet much of this labor remained "unofficial." Women continued to be essential to the war effort while being denied the standing, authority, and long-term security typically associated with service. That tension— dependence without full recognition — became a defining feature of women's Civil War experience and shaped everything that followed.

Medical Catastrophe Becomes a System: Early Battles and the Birth of Medical Infrastructure

Early battles revealed what both sides had not prepared for: mass casualties without adequate medical infrastructure.

The scale was staggering. Thousands of wounded men were arriving at field hospitals that had no beds, no bandages, and no surgeons enough to handle the flood. Makeshift operating tables set up in barns and churches. Amputated limbs piled outside tent flaps. The screaming that never stopped.

In response, a web of organizations and semi-official structures emerged. The U.S. Sanitary Commission. The Women's Central Association of Relief. These groups coordinated supplies, hospital relief, and volunteer labor at a scale the nation had never attempted before.

Women fundraised, stitched, packaged, inspected, and distributed goods—organizing "Sanitary Fairs" that raised millions of dollars, running supply depots, and auditing hospital conditions. They also pushed their way into hospital work and patient care in a military culture that often resisted them. Army surgeons and administrators didn't want women in their wards. They said women were too delicate, too emotional, and too disruptive to military order.

The women came anyway.

The Civil War nurse is often flattened into a moral symbol—the angel of mercy gliding serenely through hospital wards, bringing comfort and Christian virtue to suffering soldiers—a figure more myth than woman.

Contemporary accounts show something harsher.

Exhaustion. Filth. Overcrowding. Infection spreading through wards where men lay shoulder to shoulder on straw mattresses soaked in blood and waste. Amputations performed without anesthesia when supplies ran out. The bureaucratic grind of supply shortages—requisition forms left unanswered, bandages that never arrived, and medicines diverted or stolen.

Louisa May Alcott's Hospital Sketches—based on letters written from her wartime nursing service—remains one of the most transparent windows into hospital life and how female caregiving was both valorized and undervalued. She described the shock of her first night on duty: the smell, the sounds, the rows of wounded men who looked at her with desperate hope she had no training to fulfill. She wrote about scrubbing floors, emptying chamber pots, holding down screaming patients during surgery, and the typhoid fever that nearly killed her after just six weeks of service.

This was the reality behind the symbol. Women who worked until they collapsed. Who contracted the same diseases that killed their patients. Who fought not only to save lives but also to be recognized as capable—to be paid fairly, given authority over their own wards, and treated as professionals rather than volunteers whose presence was merely tolerated.

The medical infrastructure that emerged from this chaos—the supply networks, the hospital protocols, the recognition that nursing required skill and training—was built as much by these women's insistence as by military necessity. They didn't wait for permission. They created the systems the war required, then dared anyone to dismantle them.

Dorothea Dix

When Dorothea Dix was appointed Superintendent of Army Nurses for the Union in 1861, she professionalized women's nursing by imposing strict standards and insisting on a kind of enforced plainness—part moral gatekeeping, part protective strategy inside a male-dominated medical world that doubted women's seriousness and feared women's "impropriety."

Dorothea's rules are often mocked today, but the sharper point is this: women had to be made "safe" to be allowed near male suffering. Their credibility was tied to a narrow, surveilled version of femininity. That bargain reappears later in the military's pregnancy rules, marriage policies, and "good character" standards.

Clara Barton, "Angel of the Battlefield"

After hauling a four-mule team from Washington to the front, Clara Barton arrived at the field hospitals just as Antietam erupted on September 17, 1862—a day that would become the bloodiest in American history—and found herself standing in the midst of its uncontained slaughter.

As surgeons worked frantically to save wounded soldiers amid dwindling supplies, a bullet struck her arm and killed the man she was caring for. She didn't retreat—instead, she distributed the wagonload of bandages and supplies she had personally collected. Surprised to see a woman tending the wounded in such large numbers, the on-duty surgeon later wrote, "I thought that night if heaven ever sent out a[n] … angel, she must be one — her assistance was so timely." She was thereafter called "The Angel of the Battlefield" and traveled to Virginia, western Maryland, South Carolina, and Georgia.[1]

Clara's Civil War nursing work became famous because it was visible. Still, her more profound contribution lay in embodying a transition: women moving from private aid to organized, persistent humanitarian infrastructure.

After the Civil War, Clara carried her battlefield experience into the work of repairing what the war had broken—bodies, records, and the fragile connections between families and the dead. She discovered that thousands of letters from relatives searching for missing Union soldiers sat unanswered in government offices, their writers begging to know whether sons, husbands, and brothers were alive, imprisoned, or buried in unmarked graves.

With Abraham Lincoln's authorization, Clara established the Office of Correspondence with Friends of the Missing Men of the United States Army in 1865, effectively turning her Washington boarding house into a one-woman reconstruction agency.[2]

Over the next several years, she and a small staff answered more than 60,000 inquiries and helped determine the fate of over 20,000 soldiers, bringing long-delayed news and some measure of closure to families across the North. Her efforts were crucial at Andersonville, the notorious Confederate prison in Georgia, where she helped supervise the identification and marking of roughly 13,000 Union graves and supported the creation of a national cemetery on the site.[3]

Clara then expanded her postwar mission from healing a divided nation to building permanent relief structures. Inspired by the International Red Cross, which offered a blueprint for organized, neutral wartime aid, she volunteered during the Franco-Prussian War, helping civilians and soldiers and witnessing firsthand how a standing relief organization could respond quickly to a crisis.

Returning to the United States, she campaigned for years to persuade a skeptical federal government that such an organization was necessary in peacetime as well as in war, arguing that floods, fires, and epidemics required the same coordinated response she had improvised during the Civil War.

She founded the American Red Cross in 1881, and served as its first president, directing disaster relief and effectively carrying the ethic of her Civil War work into a national institution that reshaped how the United States handled both military and civilian emergencies.

Clara is evidence that once women proved they could build systems under pressure, they did not simply disappear. They carried wartime capacity into postwar institutions.

Clara Barton

Susie King Taylor

Beyond famous names, many other women provided nursing and medical labor in and around Union lines, often identified in records as "contraband" (escaped enslaved people). That terminology itself is revealing: it frames human beings as seized property even as they performed lifesaving service.

These women entered the Union war effort through categories the army knew how to name—"laundress," "cook," "servant"—even when their work stretched far beyond those titles. Susie King Taylor's life shows how misleading those labels could be.

Born enslaved in Georgia in 1848, she learned to read and write in secret schools run by free Black women in Savannah, absorbing literacy that was both illegal and life-changing.

When Union forces took control of parts of the South Atlantic coast early in the war, she escaped to Union lines on the Sea Islands, where her ability to read, write, and work under pressure made her immediately useful to Black regiments forming under federal authority.

Officially, Susie attached herself to the 1st South Carolina Volunteers (later redesignated the 33rd United States Colored Troops) as a laundress, one of the few roles open to Black women within army regulations. In reality, she did far more. She nursed sick and wounded soldiers in camps and field hospitals, dressing wounds, managing fevers, and sitting long hours with men whose bodies and spirits were breaking under combat, disease, and overwork.

She cooked and washed, but she also read letters aloud, helped men compose replies, and taught soldiers and refugee children to read and write around campfires and in rough shelters whenever the regiment paused long enough to make a classroom out of a corner of camp.

Her memoir, the first for a black woman, was published in 1902. It recalls moving with the unit on expeditions along the Georgia and South Carolina coasts, sharing the dangers of raids and skirmishes while tending to men who were simultaneously fighting the Confederacy and proving their right to full citizenship.

Susie's service underscores how much of Black women's wartime labor disappears behind a single word in official paperwork. "Laundress" appears in rosters and pay records because the army could recognize and grudgingly compensate that role; it was a framework never designed to accommodate a Black woman who moved fluidly between roles—nurse, teacher, confidante—serving as the steady emotional center of a Black regiment whose very existence challenged the assumptions of the age.

After the war, that tenuous space vanished. During Reconstruction and the long, tightening grip of Jim Crow, teaching was no longer an option. With few choices left, she entrusted her infant to her mother and took the only work available, entering the household of a wealthy white family as a domestic servant. In her own writing, Susie would later speak plainly of the terror that surrounded her—the routine lynchings, the laws carefully engineered to criminalize Black life and enforce white supremacy.

Even in her later years, she refused to retreat from the world's unfinished struggles. After the Spanish-American War, she turned her attention beyond the United States, seeking ways to aid Afro-Cubans navigating yet another uncertain aftermath of empire and war.

She noticed that Afro-Cubans were being discriminated against in Cuba in similar ways to African Americans in the American South during Reconstruction.

Without women like Susie King Taylor, many Civil War soldiers would have faced illness, loneliness, and bureaucratic obstacles with far less support. Her work illustrates what the army's categories obscured: that Black women's intellectual, medical, and educational work was central to the war for Union and emancipation, even when the state tried to file it away under the most modest of titles.

Susie King Taylor

Harriet Tubman: Intelligence, Scouting, and Operational Impact

While Harriet Tubman is best known for her role in the Underground Railroad, her contributions to the Civil War as a scout and intelligence gatherer are lesser known. Her wartime work pushed her beyond the already dangerous world of the Underground Railroad into formal, organized military intelligence.

During the Civil War, she traveled to Union-occupied territory in the South Carolina Sea Islands, where thousands of enslaved people had fled to federal lines and the army was learning how to wage war in a landscape of tidal rivers, rice plantations, and marsh. There, Harriet worked under Union officers as a scout, guide, and intelligence operative, drawing on skills honed over years of clandestine movement—stealth, navigation, reading people, and building trust among enslaved communities.

She traveled by boat and on foot through the waterways and plantations along the Combahee and neighboring rivers, mapping channels, noting troop positions, and, crucially, building relationships with enslaved people who could report on Confederate defenses, supply depots, and hidden river mines.

Her most famous military operation was the Combahee River Raid of June 2, 1863. Working with Colonel James Montgomery and Black troops of the 2nd South Carolina Volunteers, she helped plan a night expedition up the Combahee, using the intelligence she had gathered to guide Union gunboats past obstructions and mines and toward key rice plantations and storehouses.[4] As the boats moved upriver at dawn, Harriet reportedly stood on deck to help direct the pilots and signal which landings to hit first.

Once Union troops began landing, enslaved people who had been forewarned through her networks fled to the riverbank in large numbers. Soldiers and sailors pulled hundreds of men, women, and children aboard while Montgomery's men burned plantations, destroyed rice stores, and crippled Confederate infrastructure in the district.

By the end of the raid, an estimated 700 or more enslaved people had seized the moment to escape, and significant food and supply resources for the Confederacy along that stretch of river lay in ruins. Many of those who fled later enlisted in the United States Colored Troops, turning an intelligence-driven raid into both a liberation action and a recruitment windfall for the Union.

Harriet's presence on the expedition and her role in making it possible reveal the full scope of her wartime work: not only ferrying people to freedom one by one before the war, but also coordinating information, logistics, and local knowledge to help wage a campaign that combined emancipation and military strategy.

After the war, she struggled for decades to receive recognition or compensation for this service, a reminder that even the most daring contributions of Black women to the Union cause were often acknowledged only in retrospect, if at all.

Southern Women in a Collapsing World

For Southern women, the Civil War arrived not only as a political crisis but as a slow unraveling of daily life. Blockades, shortages, inflation, and the steady removal of men from households turned survival into a constant calculation. As the war progressed, cities and farms alike faced scarcity; enslaved labor systems destabilized; social hierarchies strained; and women were forced into unfamiliar roles as managers, providers, and negotiators with military authority.

Southern women nursed the wounded, organized hospitals, produced clothing and supplies, and endured occupation and displacement. Many also faced moral and practical dilemmas arising from slavery's collapse—whether to resist, accommodate, or exploit the changing order. Their experiences were not uniform. Class, race, and proximity to military action shaped everything from access to food to exposure to violence.

Importantly, Southern women lived under a government increasingly suspicious of dissent. Expressions of loyalty were observed, correspondence was monitored, and deviations were punished. In that environment, women's traditional invisibility could function as both protection and constraint. It was within this space—where expectation, surveillance, and necessity collided—that one of the Civil War's most effective intelligence networks took shape.

Elizabeth Van Lew and Mary Richards/Bowser

Elizabeth Van Lew was a white woman from a prominent slaveholding family who privately opposed secession. She quietly built and coordinated an information and aid system entirely within the Confederate capital of Richmond, Virginia. She and her allies smuggled food and medicine to Union prisoners, helped men escape from Libby Prison, and cultivated informants who relayed details about Confederate troop movements, fortifications, and political plans.

That network was interracial by necessity and design. It drew on free and enslaved Black Richmonders who could move through streets, markets, workshops, and white households with a degree of invisibility that white Unionists could not. Information was concealed in mundane objects, written in cipher, or memorized and passed orally. Messages moved through domestic spaces and routes that mirrored women's everyday labor and therefore escaped scrutiny. Enslaved and free Black operatives played essential roles within this network, exploiting the Confederacy's racial assumptions to move intelligence with relative freedom.

After the war, several Union officers, including General Ulysses S. Grant, acknowledged Elizabeth's contribution, describing her intelligence as exceptionally valuable to the Union cause.[5]

Some evidence suggests that a Black woman connected to Elizabeth's network was educated in the North and later returned to Richmond. This may be the figure later remembered as Mary Richards or Mary Bowser.[6]

A few scattered references hint at a woman of impressive memory and nerve who worked in a key Confederate household and fed intelligence back to the Van Lew network. But many of the specific claims that animate modern retellings—exact conversations overheard in Davis's office, detailed descriptions of dress and daring escapes—rely on reminiscences written decades later or on sources that cannot be checked against contemporary documents.

The risks were real. For these women, discovery would have meant imprisonment or execution. But they persisted anyway, sustained by conviction.

After Union forces captured Richmond in 1865, Elizabeth paid a price. In postwar Richmond, she was ostracized, financially strained, and remembered by many neighbors not as a patriot, but as a traitor. Her later appointment as postmaster—a reward for loyalty—did little to restore her standing in a city committed to forgetting internal dissent.

Elizabeth Van Lew and her network were not exceptional because they were women. They were remarkable for using social, racial, and political systems to counter a government that assumed loyalty could be read on the surface.

Think about that for a moment. They built an intelligence network that operated for years under the noses of Confederate officials who never imagined that the people serving them tea, delivering their laundry, or visiting their prisons might be counting their troops and copying their dispatches.

Her story reminds us that intelligence work often looks like ordinary life. That some of the most consequential acts of war leave the fewest visible traces. No monuments. No battle honors. Just information passed quietly from hand to hand, changing the course of campaigns in ways that would never appear in official reports.

The Civil War's unofficial army left a permanent footprint. Not just heroic stories, but institutional lessons about what war demands from women—and what the nation is willing to admit afterward.

The women who nursed, spied, organized relief efforts, ran farms and businesses, followed armies, and fled to freedom didn't wait for permission to act. They created the systems the war required, then watched as those systems were dismantled or forgotten once the fighting stopped. Their labor was essential. Their contributions were undeniable. Yet when the war ended, and the memorials went up, their names were rarely carved in stone.

What remained was a question the nation has never fully answered: If women can do this work in wartime, why not in peace? If their intelligence, their organizational skill, their physical endurance, and their moral courage are essential when the nation is in crisis, what does it mean to deny them full citizenship when the crisis passes?

The Civil War didn't resolve that question. It only made it impossible to ignore.

Confederate Women, Nursing, and the War of Scarcity

Confederate hospitals were born of scarcity. From the earliest months of the war, Southern medical infrastructure struggled under the weight of mass casualties, limited industrial capacity, and an increasingly effective Union blockade. Medications, bandages, food, clean linens, and trained personnel were perpetually scarce. Into this system stepped women—often without formal training, authority, or protection—who became essential to the Confederacy's ability to care for its wounded.

Nursing in the Confederacy was not institutionalized in the same way it was in the Union. There was no equivalent of the U.S. Sanitary Commission, and Confederate medical administration remained fragmented throughout the war. As a result, women's nursing labor was often improvised, local, and dependent on individual initiative rather than centralized planning.

One of the clearest examples of this improvisation is Sally Louisa Tompkins, a Richmond woman who used her own resources to establish a private hospital for Confederate soldiers. Her facility, later known as Robertson Hospital, earned a strong reputation for patient survival, leading Confederate authorities to grant her the rank of captain, an extraordinary exception not intended to honor women broadly but to protect her hospital from bureaucratic interference.[7]

Sally's case underscores a recurring theme: when women's work proved indispensable, institutions found ways to accommodate it—without changing the underlying rules.

Most Confederate women nurses operated far from such recognition. They worked in makeshift hospitals established in homes, churches, warehouses, and schools. Conditions were often grim: overcrowded wards, insufficient sanitation, high rates of infection, and constant shortages. Women cleaned wounds, assisted in amputations, prepared food from inadequate supplies, and sat with dying men who would never return home. Their labor blurred the line between medical care and emotional containment, absorbing grief that had no official outlet.

Class also shaped who could nurse and how. Elite white women often entered hospitals as supervisors or volunteers, leveraging social standing to gain access. Poorer women—both white and Black—were more likely to perform the most physically demanding and least acknowledged tasks: laundering blood-soaked linens, hauling water, disposing of waste, and caring for patients no one else would touch. Enslaved women, compelled into hospital labor, appear in the record only intermittently, their work documented as property use rather than service.

Another Confederate nursing account comes from Phoebe Yates Pember, who served as a matron at Chimborazo Hospital in Richmond, one of the largest military hospitals during the war.

In her later memoir, Phoebe described not only the physical toll of nursing but also the constant negotiation of authority: defending her decisions against male doctors, quartermasters, and officers who alternately relied on and resented women's presence. Her writing strips away sentiment and portrays Confederate nursing as administrative, exhausting, and politically constrained.

As the war dragged on, scarcity worsened. Inflation eroded household resources. Blockades tightened. Hospitals struggled to feed patients adequately. Nurses often supplemented rations from their own dwindling stores. Women were expected to embody sacrifice without complaint, even as the system that depended on them failed to supply basic necessities.

Phoebe Yates Pember

By the final year of the war, Confederate medical care was collapsing alongside the state itself. Yet women continued to work in hospitals until Richmond fell and facilities were abandoned or overrun. Their endurance did not translate into postwar security. Unlike Union nurses, Confederate women did not benefit from later federal pension reforms.

Their service became part of a regional memory that emphasized devotion and suffering while offering little material support.

The work of these women nurses occupies an uncomfortable space in American history. War expands women's responsibilities without increasing their authority. When the war ends, responsibility is remembered; authority is not.

The Pension System: A Blunt Instrument for a Complex War

After the war, the Union pension system became one of the most significant administrative undertakings of the postwar federal government. The foundation was the Pension Act of 1862, which expanded and standardized pension eligibility for those who served after 1861, including provisions for widows and orphans. The law is often described as remarkably "liberal" for its time, yet its "liberality" still assumed a particular model of service and dependency: the soldier was male; the widow was a dependent who had to prove legitimacy.

The paperwork requirements were not incidental—they were the policy. To obtain a widow's pension, a claimant typically had to establish marriage, death, and (depending on the era and claim type) continued eligibility, often including evidence about remarriage.

Pension files became enormous because proof was demanded, contested, and frequently resubmitted over time. The National Archives' own research guidance emphasizes the extent of these files and the personal evidence they contain.

This is where women re-enter the historical record in large numbers: not because the government tracked women's wartime work well, but because women had to fight for recognition through documents.

Widows: Grief Converted Into Evidence

The widow's pension file is a distinct kind of American source—part legal dossier, part intimate biography. It can contain affidavits from neighbors, clergy, midwives, employers, and family; marriage records; testimony about cohabitation and reputation; and details of poverty and illness that women never would have volunteered except under bureaucratic pressure. In other words, the pension system did what war histories often fail to do: it forced the state to record women's postwar lives, even if in a framework that treated them primarily as dependents.

But that framework came with a price. A widow's credibility was not simply a matter of law; it was a matter of moral judgment. The state evaluated women through a cultural lens: respectability, marital legitimacy, and continued "worthiness" could become de facto criteria. The war had killed husbands and destabilized communities; the pension system then required women to present themselves as legible and acceptable to federal authority.

Nurses: Service Performed, Status Denied

Nursing is where the postwar recognition problem is clearest. The Union relied on female nurses and large-scale relief efforts, yet most women who nursed were not integrated into the military as soldiers. Many were paid irregularly or served in volunteer roles that were later difficult to document. The nation praised them as symbols of virtue, but symbols do not automatically receive pensions.

A key shift came with the Army Nurses Pension Act of 1892, which granted pension eligibility to many women who had served as nurses. Even then, the dividing line between "official" and "volunteer" service remained a trap—women not on government payrolls faced higher hurdles to prove eligibility. Later reform efforts by nurse organizations sought to broaden and clarify access for those excluded by narrow documentation standards.

Here, the larger pattern emerges: women's wartime labor was often acceptable when it was framed as charitable, but compensation required it to be framed as state service—and the state controlled the definitions.

Harriet Tubman: Recognized, Then Required to Ask Again

Harriet Tubman's postwar struggle is one of the starkest illustrations of the recognition gap. The National Archives preserves material related to her efforts to secure compensation and a pension—documents that show both the breadth of the work she claimed (scout, nurse, cook, spy) and the long delay between service and institutional acknowledgment.[8]

Even when she received support, it arrived through an indirect channel: she was granted a pension as the widow of a Union veteran, then later sought additional compensation for her own wartime service. The Archives' education materials and features on her claim underline the central question: what, specifically, did Congress acknowledge, and why was recognition so difficult to secure?

Harriet's story is not just "a hero overlooked." It is evidence of a system in which a Black woman's service—especially service performed in intelligence and irregular roles—could be widely praised in rhetoric and still require decades of petitions to convert into material support.

Anna Ella Carroll

Postwar recognition fights were not limited to nursing and widows' claims.

Some women sought formal credit for intellectual or strategic contributions during the war, entering territory the era considered deeply and exclusively male. The realm of strategy. Of policy. Of ideas that shaped how the war was fought and justified.

Anna Ella Carroll is the clearest case of this type.

She petitioned for compensation for what she argued were substantial services to the government during the war. Not nursing. Not relief work. Not the kinds of contributions the nation had grudgingly learned to acknowledge. But intellectual labor. Strategic thinking. The work of shaping policy and planning campaigns.

Born into a politically connected Maryland family, she carved out a role as a Unionist pamphleteer whose constitutional writings bolstered Lincoln's expansive interpretation of presidential war powers. Her work was recognized by contemporaries in government as useful—even if it remained largely anonymous to the broader public.

Her influential pamphlets argued that secession was legally invalid and that the president could wield broad war powers to suppress rebellion. This theory closely paralleled and supported Abraham Lincoln's exercise of executive authority at a moment when that authority was being challenged from every direction. Her words gave constitutional cover to actions that might otherwise have been deemed tyrannical.

She also visited the Western theater in 1861 and submitted memoranda urging a Union advance along the Tennessee and Cumberland Rivers—a strategic recommendation she later insisted had shaped the successful campaign that captured Forts Henry and Donelson and opened the way to Shiloh and beyond. Whether her advice directly influenced Union strategy remains debated. What's undeniable is that she believed it did—and that she spent decades fighting for recognition of that contribution.

Her decades-long effort to secure congressional compensation—supported by thick files of petitions and promotional biographies—demonstrates how women used claims to "military and other services" to challenge not only whether they counted as participants in the war, but also whether planning, advising, and theorizing could themselves be recognized as legitimate forms of service.

Could a woman's ideas be worth paying for? Could strategic thinking—the kind of work that happened in offices and studies rather than on battlefields or in hospital wards—be acknowledged as war work when it came from a woman's pen?

Congress never fully answered those questions in Anna's favor. Her petitions were debated, tabled, revived, and ultimately denied. But the existence of these congressional documents shows a second front in the postwar battle: women challenging not only whether they served, but also what kinds of work could count as service at all.

It was one thing to acknowledge that women had nursed the wounded—that fit comfortably within existing ideas about female virtue and maternal care. It was quite another to admit that a woman might have helped plan a military campaign, or shaped the constitutional theory that justified a president's war powers, or contributed to Union victory through the force of her intellect rather than the labor of her hands.

That admission would require recognizing women not just as helpers in war, but as thinkers. Strategists. Citizens whose minds mattered as much as their service.

The nation wasn't ready for that. Not yet.

The War Women Kept Fighting

Postwar pension and compensation battles clarify what the war itself obscured: service is not only what people do. It is what the state will recognize.

The Civil War pushed women into public work on a scale the nation could not ignore. But the legal and administrative categories lagged behind reality, shaping who received security in old age, who received care for disability, and who appeared in the record as a legitimate participant in national sacrifice.

By the late nineteenth century, the pension system expanded dramatically in scope and cost, becoming a major public program. But that expansion did not automatically correct women's exclusion; instead, it often amplified the burden of proof placed on those whose work was informal, volunteer, coerced, or not filed under the right label.

Women's wartime labor was still easier to praise than to pay for—especially when it did not fit cleanly into payroll records and military categories.

The Civil War created a template for the next century: women would serve, the nation would rely on them, and then—through pensions, policies, and public memory—women would have to fight again to make that service count.

[1] "Clara Barton," National Museum of the United States Army; "Angel of the Battlefield: Humanitarian Clara Barton," Arlington Public Library.
[2] "Clara Barton," National Museum of the United States Army; "Clara Barton's Story: The Missing Soldiers Office, 1865–1868," Clara Barton Missing Soldiers Office Museum.
[3] Susie King Taylor, Reminiscences of My Life in Camp with the 33d United States Colored Troops, Late 1st S.C. Volunteers (Boston: Published by the Author, 1902), 5–7.
[4] "The Combahee Ferry Raid," National Museum of African American History and Culture; "Combahee River Raid (June 2, 1863)," BlackPast.org.
[5] Elizabeth R. Varon, Southern Lady, Yankee Spy: The True Story of Elizabeth Van Lew, a Union Agent in the Heart of the Confederacy (New York: Oxford University Press, 2003), esp. 237–42.
[6] Mary Richards Bowser (fl. 1846–1867)," Encyclopedia Virginia.
[7] "Sally Louisa Tompkins," Virginia Changemakers, Library of Virginia; "Sally Tompkins—Confederate Nurse," American Civil War Museum.
[8] "Claim of Harriet Tubman," National Archives; "Congress and Harriet Tubman's Claim for a Pension," National Archives.

Part III — The World Wars

Chapter 4 — World War I and the Administrative Army

✲✲

"The world was mad, and the war made it worse."

— Vera Brittain

WORLD WAR I (1914–1918) began as a European war rooted in imperial rivalry, rigid alliances, and militarized nationalism, and rapidly escalated into the first global industrial conflict on an unprecedented scale. Sparked by the assassination of Archduke Franz Ferdinand in the summer of 1914, the crisis activated binding diplomatic and military commitments that drew the major European powers into mass mobilization, trench warfare, and mechanized killing on a scale the world had never seen.

What began as a regional dispute in the Balkans became a continental catastrophe within weeks. Armies that had planned swift, decisive campaigns found themselves locked in a grinding stalemate. Men dug into the earth and stayed there—for months, then years—while artillery turned the landscape into a moonscape of mud, craters, and barbed wire.

When the United States entered the war in 1917, it joined a conflict already defined by vast conscripted armies, economies retooled for total war, and civilians increasingly absorbed into the material and emotional burdens of combat. This was not a war of professional soldiers and distant battles. It was a war that demanded everything: every factory, every farm, every able-bodied person, every ounce of national will.

The war eroded older distinctions between the battlefront and the home front.

Governments built sprawling administrative, medical, logistical, and communications apparatuses that demanded labor far beyond what traditional military structures could supply. Armies needed millions of uniforms, billions of rounds of ammunition, mountains of food, fleets of trucks and ambulances, and hospitals that could process casualties by the trainload. They needed telephone operators who could route calls under fire, clerks who could track supplies across continents, and nurses who could work in conditions that would have broken earlier generations.

They needed women.

Victory came at staggering human costs—millions dead, empires collapsed, a generation of young men lost to the trenches—and decisively reshaped international politics. The map of Europe was redrawn. Old dynasties fell. New nations emerged from the wreckage.

But the war also transformed the conduct and organization of war, creating new institutional spaces in which women's labor became indispensable and conspicuous, and—though still uneven and incomplete—was at last formally recognized.

For the first time in American history, women were not just tolerated on the margins of military life or acknowledged quietly for their contributions. They were recruited. Uniformed. Given rank and pay, and sent overseas in organized units with official status. The military created new categories—yeomanettes, marinettes, Hello Girls—to accommodate their presence, even as it struggled to define what that presence meant.

This was not equality. Not yet. But it was a crack in the foundation of a system that had always insisted women had no place in the machinery of war. And once that crack appeared, it could never be fully sealed again.

World War I: Nurses and the Medical Corps

When the United States entered World War I, the Army's medical system expanded faster than its staffing could keep pace.

The Army Nurse Corps existed before 1917, but it was not designed for a war that produced industrial-scale casualties, mass evacuation chains, and prolonged hospital backlogs. Within months, nursing became one of the most urgent manpower problems for the American Expeditionary Forces (AEF): wounded men arrived in surges, surgeons worked with limited supplies, and hospitals—at home and overseas—needed trained personnel immediately.

The scale of the response was unprecedented. Across the war, roughly 22,000 nurses served, with slightly over 10,000 overseas in the AEF.[1]

By late 1918, Army nursing strength had reached the tens of thousands, and the work was not confined to a single setting: nurses served in base and evacuation hospitals, on hospital trains, and aboard transport ships carrying wounded men across the Atlantic.

This was not the romantic image of nursing. It was war work under pressure—long shifts, constant triage, and the unglamorous mechanics of sustaining life inside overcrowded wards. Nurses cared for men with catastrophic wounds and shock; they managed infection control at the edge of what early twentieth-century medicine could reliably prevent; and they worked within a hierarchy that granted them responsibility without full military authority.

The system treated nursing as "women's work," but the war treated it as a strategic necessity.

The result was a grim arithmetic repeated throughout this book: when war expands women's roles, it also expands women's exposure to danger—often without expanding their formal status.

Helen Fairchild, Base Hospital No. 10

Helen Fairchild was not a career soldier, but World War I turned her into something close to one: a medical professional operating inside an industrial war machine that treated exhaustion, exposure, and attrition as routine. A Pennsylvania Hospital graduate, she volunteered with the hospital's unit—U.S. Base Hospital No. 10—one of the early American medical contingents to deploy to Europe in 1917.

In France, Helen's work quickly moved beyond the relative safety of a rear-area ward. She was assigned to a British casualty clearing station near Ypres, where the war's wounded arrived in relentless waves and where hospitals were close enough to the front to be shelled and bombed. Accounts of her service emphasize that she nursed large numbers of gas casualties under fire—precisely the kind of proximity that collapses the comforting distinction between "front line" and "support."

Her wartime letters to her family were widely noted for their clarity about conditions and the emotional and physical toll of combat nursing. Those letters—like many women's war records—became part of the archive not because the military prioritized women's voices, but because women wrote anyway, and families preserved what the state did not.[2]

She became seriously ill while still on duty, underwent surgery in January 1918, and died in France days later.

Contemporary and later accounts record her cause of death as acute yellow atrophy of the liver while serving with Base Hospital No. 10. In other words, she died the way modern wars often kill medical workers—through cumulative damage, disease, and medical limitations rather than a single dramatic moment.

Helen's postwar legacy is revealing in its own right. She is remembered as a nurse who "served" rather than a veteran who "fought," even though her work placed her under bombardment and amid chemical warfare casualties.

Her letters survived; her status remained ambiguous.

Segregation: Policy, Not Practice

World War I expanded American military nursing at a scale the United States had never attempted before, but that expansion was not evenly open to all women. Race shaped who could enter official channels, where women could serve, and how their service was remembered afterward.

For most of World War I, Black American nurses were excluded from the U.S. military nursing system—not because they lacked training, but because segregation was institutionalized as policy. Many were credentialed and willing to serve, and the American Red Cross certified large numbers for potential wartime service, yet the Army Nurse Corps and related channels largely refused to accept them until the crisis became unmanageable.

That moment arrived with the 1918 influenza pandemic. Nursing placed women directly in the path of contagion, and the pandemic intensified both workload and risk, especially in crowded hospitals and camps. Contemporary military history accounts and cemetery/historical summaries document that influenza became a major crisis among American medical staff overseas and that special infirmaries and convalescent arrangements were created as nurses themselves fell ill.

The Eighteen

As influenza tore through military camps and hospitals, the Army's need for nurses collided with its own discrimination. Under mounting pressure and emergency conditions, the Army and the Red Cross finally accepted a small group of Black nurses—eighteen women—for service in 1918–1919.[3] They were assigned to central U.S. training installations, including Camp Grant (Illinois) and Camp Sherman (Ohio), at the height of a public-health catastrophe that overwhelmed staff, beds, and supplies.

Their assignment did not erase segregation; it carried it with them. The "Eighteen" served within a system that often enforced separate living arrangements and treated their presence as an exception granted in an emergency rather than a right earned through qualification. In practice, they performed the same essential wartime nursing labor required everywhere in 1918: triage, bedside care, infection control as early twentieth-century medicine could manage, and the relentless work of keeping sick soldiers alive in overcrowded facilities.

The significance is not only what they did—it is the logic the state revealed while using them: exclusion until desperation; inclusion without equality; then removal when the emergency passed.

That removal came quickly. After the crisis and demobilization, the Army Nurse Corps discharged these nurses in 1919, and the door narrowed again. Yet their service mattered beyond the weeks and months they worked in influenza wards. It established a documented precedent that Black nurses could be integrated into military nursing when the institution chose to recognize them—an argument that would reappear in later conflicts, especially World War II.

Indigenous women, by contrast, appear in even smaller numbers in the Army Nurse Corps record, but their presence is documented, including service overseas. The result is a familiar wartime pattern: need temporarily widened access, while postwar institutions kept recognition narrow and uneven.

Cora Elm (Oneida) — Nursing Overseas in the AEF

Cora Elm, a member of the Oneida Nation, trained as a nurse and volunteered for wartime service when the United States entered the conflict. She is consistently identified in institutional accounts as one of the 14 Indigenous women

who served in the Army Nurse Corps during World War I—
and among the small number who served overseas with the
American Expeditionary Forces.[4]

Born on the Oneida Reservation in Wisconsin, she was one
of eleven children and the granddaughter of Jacob Hill, a
hereditary chief of the Oneida Nation. She left for Europe
in late 1917 and served at a base hospital in France, where
the work was less glamorous than the word "base"
suggests. She spent roughly nine months at a base hospital
that treated over 9,000 patients, a statistic that conveys
what her service actually meant—high-volume medical
labor under wartime strain.

Cora Elm

"My life overseas was not very easy. Although I was in a base hospital, I saw a lot of the horrors of war. I nursed many a soldier with a leg cut off, or an arm", she later wrote.

Her return to civilian life included the era's typical expectations, such as marriage and a son. However, she remained committed to service and worked as a nurse after the war, including posts at Fort Bayard Hospital in New Mexico and Wood Veterans Hospital in Milwaukee, where she supervised tuberculosis wards. She divorced and died in 1949 at the age of 58.

The "Hello Girls"

Modern war ran on wires. By 1917, the telephone had become a central tool of military command—faster than messengers, more flexible than written dispatches, and essential for coordinating artillery, logistics, and rapidly shifting front-line decisions.

But the American Expeditionary Forces (AEF) arrived in France with a communications problem: too few trained operators and a language barrier that slowed or distorted orders. General John J. Pershing requested bilingual (French/English) telephone operators to improve communications on the Western Front.

The Army's solution was radical for its time and immediately revealing: it recruited women.

Sworn In, Uniformed, Deployed

The unit formally known as the Signal Corps Female Telephone Operators Unit—later nicknamed the "Hello Girls"—recruited from thousands of applicants; 223 women were accepted and sent to France to operate switchboards for the U.S. Army.[5]

Their work was not decorative clerical labor. They connected and routed calls that transmitted operational decisions throughout the American military system in France, often under pressure and sometimes near combat zones. They served in uniform, under Army direction, within the Army communications infrastructure—conditions most people would assume define military service. Even today, museums preserve their Signal Corps uniforms as military artifacts because, visually and practically, that is what this work was.

The Machine's Human Operators

Their recruitment criteria reveal the modernity of the war: the Army needed not just "women" but skilled professionals—experienced switchboard operators who could work quickly, under stress, and in two languages. The popular nickname "Hello Girls" drew on the existing cultural association of women with telephone work, but in France, these operators became part of the combat infrastructure: the human interface between command intent and battlefield execution.

While earlier wars relied on women's labor in ways that remained semi-formal—laundresses, nurses, camp followers —World War I institutionalized women in technical war systems: communications, records, routing, and coordination. It brought women into the machinery that made mass mobilization possible.

"Not Soldiers" (Until Decades Later)

Then came the familiar postwar turn: classification.

Despite being sworn in and deployed by the Army, the Hello Girls were treated after the war as civilian contract employees rather than veterans. They did not receive the status and benefits extended to recognized military personnel, and many spent decades trying to have their service acknowledged as what it had been in practice: Army service.

Six members of the U.S. Army Signal Corps, 1918

Congress later summarized what happened with unusual clarity: President Jimmy Carter signed the GI Bill Improvement Act of 1977 (Public Law 95–202), which allowed the surviving Signal Corps telephone operators to receive veteran status in 1979. This timeline is not a footnote; it is the point. The war needed them immediately, yet the state took far longer to provide recognition and compensation.

Grace Banker

Before the war, Grace Banker was already an experienced telephone supervisor—precisely the skilled professional that modern warfare required but did not yet know how to classify.

When the U.S. Army Signal Corps recruited women operators in 1918, Grace was selected not only to serve, but to lead. She became the chief operator of the Signal Corps Female Telephone Operators Unit, responsible for managing personnel, maintaining performance standards, and ensuring communications functioned under battlefield conditions. Her assignment placed her at the center of the American Expeditionary Forces' communications network in France.

Once in England, Grace and her unit boarded a ferry bound for France, only to find themselves stalled in the Channel. Bad weather rolled in, followed by a dense fog that refused to lift. Unable to make landfall, the vessel dropped anchor a few miles offshore. For forty-eight hours, they remained on deck, exposed to wind and cold, waiting for the coast to reappear.

The delay did not break their spirits. Looking back, Grace marveled at the composure of the women around her—how readily they accepted discomfort as the price of being first. "What good sports girls were in that First Unit," she wrote. "They took everything in their stride. They were the pioneers."

That resilience would be tested again and again. Grace and her operators worked through German bombing raids, endured brutal weather without heat, and slept in barracks that leaked as steadily as the rain outside. It was not the war they had imagined, but it was the war they had come to serve.

They worked long shifts routing calls that carried operational orders, artillery coordination, and logistical decisions. Speed and accuracy were not abstract virtues; mistakes could delay movements or misdirect resources. Unlike clerical work performed after the fact, telephone operations occurred in real time, under stress, and often near active combat zones.

She did not carry a rifle. She had the war on a wire—and the Army depended on her to keep it moving.

Contemporary accounts describe her enforcing discipline, training operators, and maintaining morale in an environment defined by fatigue and urgency. Her leadership was recognized during the war itself. In 1919, she received the Distinguished Service Medal from the U.S. Army—the only woman Signal Corps operator to receive that honor—for her "exceptionally meritorious and distinguished services." The language of the citation is telling: the Army acknowledged her work as essential, even exemplary.

And yet, like the women she commanded, Grace was not classified as a soldier when the war ended.

After demobilization, she returned to civilian life without veteran status, benefits, or the institutional recognition that would normally accompany such a decoration. The contradiction was stark. The Army had trusted her to manage a critical wartime system, awarded her for excellence, and then categorized her service out of existence.

World War I did not merely expand women's participation in war; it professionalized it, and their exclusion from formal status was not a reflection of capability or contribution, but of institutional reluctance to adjust definitions.

Yeoman (F) "Yeomanettes" — Enlisted Women in the Navy

When the Navy confronted wartime manpower shortages, it did something the Army had not yet done at scale: it enlisted women as sailors. The legal opening came from the

Naval Reserve Act of 1916, which authorized enlistment of qualified "persons" rather than explicitly "men."

In March 1917—weeks before the United States entered the war—Secretary of the Navy Josephus Daniels approved women's enlistment as Yeoman (F) ("F" for female).

Why the Navy Wanted Women

The purpose was blunt and practical: women could replace men in shore-based clerical work, allowing more men to be reassigned to sea duty and wartime operations. Yeomen handled the Navy's paper backbone—orders, correspondence, personnel records, pay documents, requisitions, and routing. In an industrial war, this administrative work was not peripheral; it was how mobilization functioned.

The scale was significant. Navy histories describe the Yeoman (F) program growing to about 11,000 women by war's end.[6]

Uniforms, Quarters, and What the Navy Hadn't Considered

Enlisting women created immediate infrastructure problems: where women would live on naval stations, how they would be supervised, and what they would wear. The Navy had no existing protocol for women on bases, forcing many Yeoman (F) to improvise living arrangements—

YWCA housing, rented rooms, shared apartments, or nearby family.

Early on, there was also no real precedent for a female enlisted uniform, and wartime expansion forced the service to formalize what had begun as improvisation. Regulations eventually specified blue or white uniforms, built around a single-breasted "Norfolk"-style jacket and a skirt with a mandated hemline, along with standardized hats and accessories that evolved as the war progressed.

Yeomanettes, World War I

Not Just Secretaries

Although the program began as clerical substitution, wartime needs expanded the Navy's requirements. While still primarily shore-based, Yeomanettes served not only as clerks but also as radio and telegraph operators, draftsmen, and other technical and logistical personnel. Although the Navy treated them as "support," they were paid, uniformed, and subject to discipline, yet still limited in where they could serve (generally not at sea).

Postwar, however, the program was demobilized, and women were pushed out as the Navy returned to peacetime norms. The institution had used women to scale the wartime workforce, then treated that inclusion as temporary.

The Intelligence Revolution

The Great War's intelligence revolution turned espionage from a scattered, ad hoc practice into a permanent part of modern warfare.

Before 1914, spying was often the work of individual agents, adventurers, and informants operating with minimal oversight and uncertain support. Intelligence gathering was improvised and unreliable, and military commanders frequently ignored it, trusting their own instincts more than shadowy reports from the field.

World War I changed everything.

The war pushed governments to build formal intelligence services, create large spy networks behind enemy lines, and professionalize codebreaking and counterespionage—laying the groundwork for structures that would define twentieth-century spying. What had been marginal became central. What had been disreputable became essential.

World War I became a turning point because industrial war demanded timely information on enemy troop movements, logistics, and morale on a scale no previous conflict had required. Armies numbering in the millions, stretched across hundreds of miles of front, and supplied by rail networks that moved thousands of tons of materiel every day—this kind of warfare couldn't be fought blind. Commanders needed to know where the enemy was massing troops, when supplies were running low, whether morale was cracking, and which sectors were vulnerable.

States responded by expanding military intelligence staffs and integrating aerial photography, signals interception, and human intelligence into a coordinated system. They began treating espionage as a legitimate tool of national policy rather than a marginal or disreputable sideline. Intelligence officers gained rank, budgets, and institutional permanence. Spy networks were organized with the same bureaucratic rigor as supply chains.

As the war dragged on, intelligence services became more bureaucratic and technical, standardizing procedures for recruiting and managing agents. They refined cryptography, developing increasingly sophisticated codes and the methods to break them. They used new technologies—radio, telegraph, aircraft—as both targets and tools for collection. Wireless intercepts could reveal enemy positions. Aerial photographs could map trench systems down to the last machine-gun nest. Captured documents could expose the entire order of battle.

This professionalization also spurred an equally intense wave of counterespionage and "spy mania."

Governments policed civilians with new ferocity, screening foreigners, monitoring mail and telegrams, and passing harsh security and secrecy laws to control information flows on the home front. Anyone with an accent, anyone who traveled frequently, anyone whose loyalty seemed even slightly questionable could find themselves under surveillance—or worse. Paranoia became policy. The hunt for spies became a tool for suppressing dissent, controlling populations, and justifying ever-greater intrusions into private life.

By the time the armistice was signed in 1918, the intelligence apparatus built during the war had become too valuable to dismantle. The networks, techniques, and institutional knowledge—all of it remained in place, ready to be reactivated. The age of modern espionage had begun, and it would never end.

Mata Hari: Myth and Reality

Mata Hari, born Margaretha Zelle, became the era's most famous alleged spy: a Dutch exotic dancer and courtesan accused of passing secrets to Germany. She moved in elite circles across prewar Europe. During the war, both German and French intelligence services made contact with her, blurring the line between opportunistic informant and professional agent.

French authorities arrested her in 1917, tried her before a military court, and convicted her of espionage, allegedly responsible for tens of thousands of French deaths.[7] However, surviving records show the evidence was fragmentary and circumstantial. That didn't matter at the time. She was executed by firing squad near Paris in October 1917. Historians have argued that she functioned more as a symbol—scapegoat, warning, and sensational story than as a demonstrably effective spy.

Louise de Bettignies and the Alice Network

Louise de Bettignies, by contrast, embodied the complex, unglamorous reality of wartime intelligence work behind German lines. A multilingual Frenchwoman recruited by British intelligence, she operated under the alias "Alice Dubois" and built an underground network, often called the Alice Network, comprising roughly 80–100 agents who gathered intelligence in occupied Belgium and northern France.[8]

Her organization tracked German troop trains, mapped gun batteries and depots, and relayed reports to British handlers through couriers and neutral-country routes.

Contemporary estimates credit the network with saving hundreds, possibly more than a thousand, Allied soldiers by warning of impending operations.

She was arrested in 1915, condemned for espionage, and died in prison in 1918. She was later commemorated as the "Queen of Spies" for demonstrating that women could run large, disciplined intelligence systems under extreme danger.

How Espionage Actually Worked

Behind the headlines, the Great War's spycraft relied on training, tradecraft, and communication methods that blended older practices with new technology. Recruits—men and women—learned to observe rail lines and troop movements, sketch maps, memorize details, use simple codes or ciphers, and maintain cover stories that matched their social positions, whether as domestic servants, railway workers, or shopkeepers.

Communication methods ranged from traditional invisible ink, microphotography, and dead drops to more systematic use of coded letters sent through regular post and carefully routed courier chains. Networks like the Alice Network and La Dame Blanche relied on dense human webs tied into Allied intelligence centers.

At the same time, parallel advances in radio interception and cryptanalysis turned the "secret war" into a more scientific enterprise in which encrypted signals, not just human couriers, carried the most valuable secrets.

Breaking the War's Messages: The Birth of American Codebreaking

World War I was the first American war fought in a sky filled with radio signals, not just paper orders and hand-carried dispatches. Once commands and intelligence began to travel through the air, they could also be intercepted—and that turned radio into a new battlefield, where the advantage went not only to those who could send messages securely but also to those who could secretly read the enemy's.

The United States entered the conflict with almost no formal codebreaking infrastructure of its own. The Army's Military Intelligence Division hastily built a small in-house code and cipher section, known as MI-8. At the same time, the government turned to civilian experts to train personnel and analyze intercepted traffic.

At least 12 women worked as cryptanalysts in MI-8, and five women at Riverbank Laboratories analyzed government material, including Elizabeth Friedman, who also taught cipher courses in late 1917. From the outset, U.S. codebreaking relied on women's labor, even as official narratives kept women largely offstage.

Agnes Meyer Driscoll ("Madame X")

Agnes Meyer Driscoll, celebrated as the "First Lady of Naval Cryptology," began her government cryptologic work during the war years, gaining training and experience in the small, improvised U.S. codebreaking world that formed around the conflict. Those early classrooms and makeshift offices—part training pipeline, part experimental lab—transformed cryptology from a niche curiosity into a national-security requirement, and Agnes moved with that transition.[9]

The work was technical, not theatrical. Cryptanalysis rewarded pattern recognition, persistence, and mathematical discipline—skills that looked gender-neutral on paper but were filtered through workplaces that still treated authority and advancement as male.

However, women remained "usable" when expertise was scarce. In World War I and its aftermath, the United States needed qualified codebreakers more than it needed to protect older assumptions about who belonged in military intelligence, opening doors just wide enough for women like Agnes to step through—if not to be fully seen.

Women Inside the National Machine—Munitions, Shipyards, and Hazardous Work

Once the United States entered World War I in 1917, the conflict became a national production project, with steel, explosives, uniforms, vehicles, wiring, food processing, and shipbuilding manufactured at speed and scale. The "home front" was not a metaphor. It was a labor system mobilized to feed the front.

Women moved into that system in numbers large enough to reshape whole sectors. The Library of Congress's WWI exhibition notes that more than one million women found skilled temporary employment in factories and offices during the war, often shifting from domestic service and other prewar work into industrial and administrative roles.

Dangerous Work

Industrial war demanded speed, and speed in early twentieth-century manufacturing carried a predictable cost: long hours, fatigue, injury, and exposure to toxic substances. "Munitions" was not a single job; it was an ecosystem—handling powders, assembling shells, operating heavy machinery, packing, and transporting.

Shipyards and metal trades added their own dangers: cranes, rivets, heat, noise, and relentless physical strain. Even where women's work was described as "lighter," the conditions were frequently harsh, and the pace was driven by wartime urgency rather than workplace safety.

The U.S. Department of Labor's Women in Service (the precursor to the Women's Bureau) issued "Standards for the Employment of Women in Industry" in 1918, a signal that women's industrial work had become not an exception but a national policy concern—hours, working conditions, and the basic fact of women's mass participation.

Katherine Stinson: The Pilot That Wasn't Allowed to Fly

World War I transformed aviation from a novelty into a necessity in months. What began as aircraft used for reconnaissance and observation quickly evolved into a critical element of modern warfare—used for artillery spotting, aerial photography, bombing, and air-to-air combat. Aircraft design advanced rapidly under wartime pressure, while pilot training and airfield construction expanded at unprecedented speed.

In the United States, military aviation operated under the Army's Signal Corps and later the Air Service, reflecting both the importance of flight and the institutional uncertainty surrounding it.

Aviation remained dangerous, experimental, and heavily stratified, even as it proved essential to battlefield coordination and morale. Within this rapidly expanding, high-risk system—desperate for skill yet conservative about authority—women like Katherine Stinson encountered the limits of what the military would permit, even as it relied on their abilities.

Katherine Stinson entered World War I as exactly the kind of asset the United States needed: an experienced pilot, flight instructor, mechanic, and public celebrity who could fly long distances and handle high-risk aviation in an era when that still took unusual skill.

Born in 1891 in Alabama, Katherine learned to fly in her early twenties at the Wright School and earned her pilot's license in 1912, becoming one of the first licensed female pilots in the United States. What set her apart was not novelty but skill.

She specialized in long-distance flights, precision flying, and public exhibitions at a time when aviation was still lethal and experimental. By her mid-twenties, she was among the highest-paid aviators in the country, flying nationally and internationally, winning races, and performing at major air meets.

She did not present herself as a curiosity; she presented herself as a professional. Newspapers covered her flights seriously, aviation journals respected her competence, and crowds came because she could do what few others—men or women—could do reliably.

She tried to put those skills directly into military service— and was refused. Katherine responded by finding the gaps between what the state would allow and what it urgently needed to be done. Using her celebrity and aircraft, she conducted publicity flights in support of wartime fundraising and Red Cross work. The best-documented example is her multi-stop flight, culminating in Washington, D.C., where she delivered a $2 million check to Treasury Secretary William G. McAdoo—money raised through war-related fundraising flights.[10]

She also pushed for something practical: an aerial ambulance corps that would use aircraft to transport wounded troops more quickly and smoothly than ground ambulances. The idea was ahead of its time, and she offered her skills to the Red Cross overseas to help establish it, but the effort was not adopted.

In late 1918, Katherine went overseas as part of the Red Cross ambulance service and traveled to Europe in October 1918, just as the war and the influenza pandemic collided. She became ill with influenza while in France, and after returning to the States, she entered a sanitarium to recuperate from tuberculosis, and her flying career effectively ended.

Katherine's story is not a simple tale of "a brave woman pilot." She personifies how the military could celebrate women's skills, use women's labor to mobilize money and morale, and still refuse to grant women the authority that matched their competence. When the institution said "no," she served around it. When she served around it, the costs were still hers to carry.

The Yeomanettes, nurses, codebreakers, and women like Cora Elm, Katherine Stinson, and Agnes Meyer Driscoll proved women could be integrated as uniformed personnel when the military chose to be pragmatic. The lasting question was whether wartime pragmatism would become permanent policy—or remain a reversible exception.

[1] "World War I," U.S. Army Medical Department Center of History and Heritage; "American Nurses in World War I," American Experience, PBS.
[2] "Nurse Helen Fairchild: My Aunt, My Hero"; American Association for the History of Nursing, "Helen Fairchild."
[3] Darlene Clark Hine et al., "The Eighteen of 1918–1919: Black Nurses and the Great Flu Pandemic in the United States," American Journal of Public Health 108, no. 11 (2018); "African American Women and WWI," National WWI Museum and Memorial.
[4] "Cora Elm," National Museum of the United States Army; "On the Western Front: Two Iroquois Nurses in World War I," American Indian magazine.
[5] "The Hello Girls of World War I—Heeding the Call," Library of Congress, April 21, 2021.
[6] "Historical Overview of Yeomen (F)," Naval History and Heritage Command; "Yeomanettes Paved the Way for Women of All Navy Ratings Today," U.S. World War I Centennial Commission.
[7] French Ministry of War, Conseil de Guerre records concerning Margaretha Geertruida Zelle (Mata Hari), 1917.
[8] Louise Marie Jeanne Henriette de Bettignies, 1914–1918 Online: International Encyclopedia of the First World War; "Louise de Bettignies," University of Lille.
[9] Thomas Coulson, The Queen of Spies: Louise de Bettignies (London: Constable, 1935).
[10] "Remembering Katherine Stinson Otero, Early Aviation Pioneer," U.S. Department of Veterans Affairs, and "Katherine Stinson," National Aviation Hall of Fame.

Chapter 5 —Total War: World War II

"The ground they broke has hard soil indeed, but with great heart and true grit, they plowed right through the prejudice and presumption, cutting a path for all women who would serve."

— Inscription for the Military Women's Memorial

WORLD WAR II (1939–1945) was a sprawling, global catastrophe that engulfed Europe, Asia, Africa, and the world's oceans, driven by expansionist dictatorships, clashing ideologies, and the collapse of the fragile order built after World War I.

After the Japanese attack on Pearl Harbor in December 1941, the United States entered a conflict that demanded nothing less than full mobilization of factories and shipyards, research labs and intelligence bureaus, railroads and cargo fleets, and the millions of workers who kept them running.

As the war intensified, the old line between "front line" and "home front" effectively disappeared: assembly lines became as critical as supply convoys, decoding rooms as consequential as command posts, and hospitals and training camps as decisive as beaches and battlefields. Victory depended not only on firepower and battlefield courage, but on the ability to choreograph people, information, and production on a scale no state had ever attempted before.

Within this vast war machine, women were no longer treated as a temporary supplement to male labor but as an operational necessity. They were formally recruited, given serial numbers and job classifications, placed in uniformed auxiliaries and civilian corps, and assigned to posts according to bureaucratic need and strategic priority—while still being held behind carefully preserved boundaries that limited their authority, denied them permanence, and muted or delayed their claims to full recognition.

Uniformed Women at Scale: WAC, WAVES, SPARS, and the Women Marines

World War II finally forced the United States to do what it had only partially tried in World War I: integrate women into the armed forces at scale, not as informal helpers or temporary substitutes, but as a managed workforce within the military bureaucracy.

The shift was not ideological. It was operational. The war needed bodies—trained, disciplined, and trackable—and the military needed a way to expand capacity without breaking its own combat rules. The result was a set of women's programs that were both groundbreaking and tightly controlled.

The Women's Army Corps (WAC) brought women into the Army's administrative and technical backbone—clerical work, communications, logistics, motor pools, supply, and a growing list of specialized assignments that freed men for combat. The WAC's very existence institutionalized a pattern visible for centuries, that women did not need permission to be useful; the state needed a structure to use them efficiently. In practice, WAC service meant uniforms, ranks, training, regulations, inspections, and the daily reality of being held to military discipline while operating in roles still framed as "support."

The Navy followed with the WAVES (Women Accepted for Volunteer Emergency Service), placing women into shore-based naval work that kept the war machine running: personnel administration, communications, coding and decoding, transport coordination, aviation administration, and clerical-heavy operations that were crucial in a global maritime war. The Coast Guard created the SPARS, and the Marine Corps formed the Women's Reserve, each drawing women into military systems that had previously depended on male labor for every function.

What these programs shared was not simply patriotism or opportunity, but boundaries. Women were brought in to expand capacity, then channeled into assignments the services could justify as necessary yet non-combatant. They wore uniforms and held rank, but their inclusion was designed to be reversible: wartime expansion without a guarantee of permanence.

The programs also carried the era's racial hierarchy into uniform. Black women were admitted in limited numbers and often assigned to segregated units or constrained by discriminatory policies. The war widened access, but it did not erase inequality—it reorganized it. World War II created unprecedented openings for women, but it also imposed unequal terms of participation.

In earlier conflicts, women appear as essential labor that institutions struggle to name. In World War II, the institution names them—WAC, WAVES, SPARS, Women Marines—and then builds rules around them.

If uniforms and rank were the visible face of women's wartime service, intelligence work was the invisible one—where women handled secrets, codes, and information that shaped operations while leaving minimal trace in public memory.

Home-Front Intelligence: Censors, Code Rooms, and the Women Who Managed Secrets

World War II turned information into a weapon on the home front. The United States did not only fight overseas; it built domestic systems to control what could be said, sent, and intercepted—because modern war ran on communications, and communications could leak.

The federal government created the Office of Censorship, which oversaw censorship of international communications and coordinated a broad wartime effort to prevent militarily useful information from reaching enemies. The National Archives' descriptions of Office of Censorship records make clear the scale and seriousness of this work, including technical operations, case histories, and intercepted communications flagged as suspicious.

The Censorship Workforce

Censorship was not glamorous. It was repetitive, procedural, and mentally exhausting—reading, extracting, summarizing, and flagging patterns. But it was intelligence work in the most literal sense: turning private communications into actionable signals about risk, violation, or espionage.

WWII's domestic intelligence machine required workers who could follow rules, maintain secrecy, and endure monotony—roles in which women were frequently recruited and relied upon, even as the public image of intelligence remained male. Technical operations, counter-espionage case histories, and the indexing of suspicious communications were daily tasks.

Arlington Hall: "Code Girls" and the War's Hidden Math

If censorship was about stopping leaks, cryptanalysis was about reading the enemy. Two of the most essential home-front intelligence centers were Arlington Hall Station, where the U.S. Army's Signal Intelligence Service (SIS) employed large numbers of women as cryptologic workers, later often called the "Code Girls," and Bletchley Park, the cryptology center for Britain. By the middle of World War

II, they were working in deliberate coordination rather than in isolation.

In 1940, the SIS was a small and largely unknown unit tasked with attacking foreign codes, and approximately 7,000 of the 10,500 staff were female. Recruited from universities, teaching posts, banks, and even finishing schools, these women arrived by train with vague instructions and secrecy oaths, then disappeared into a world of locked doors, cover stories, and relentless shifts. They were told only that the job was vital and that they could not speak of it, not to parents, not to friends, not even to one another across sections.

Genevieve Grotjan Feinstein and the "Purple" Break

Hired for the SIS in 1939, Genevieve Grotjan Feinstein made the discovery that led to breaking the Japanese diplomatic cipher known as "Purple."[1]

Trained in mathematics and working as a statistician, in an office filled with cigarette smoke, scratch paper, and endless streams of enciphered characters, she joined a team trying to solve an especially stubborn problem: the new Japanese high-level diplomatic cipher, which American cryptanalysts nicknamed "Purple."

The job looked nothing like the glamorous espionage of popular imagination. It meant poring over pages of intercepted messages, searching for patterns buried so deep that most eyes could not see them.

"Purple" itself was a machine-based cipher system used by the Japanese Foreign Ministry to encrypt its most sensitive diplomatic traffic between Tokyo and its embassies. Unlike older manual codes, Purple relied on an electro-mechanical device that permuted letters through complex wiring paths, producing encipherments that shifted in ways that did not repeat in any obvious cycle.

For SIS, this meant that familiar techniques used on earlier Japanese systems no longer worked cleanly. They knew the messages were diplomatic; they could see the traffic flow, but the underlying system remained opaque. Breaking Purple required someone to recognize hidden structure in what looked like pure noise.

That recognition came from Genevieve. After months of studying intercepted messages, she noticed particular regularities in letter substitutions—tiny, statistical "tugs" that suggested the cipher machine did not scramble the alphabet as randomly as it appeared. On a summer afternoon in 1940, she saw the key clearly. Colleagues later recalled her literally running down the hall with her discovery.

Her insight allowed SIS engineers to design and build a functional analog of the Japanese machine without ever having seen the original hardware. Once that replica existed, American cryptanalysts could begin reading a significant portion of Japanese high-level diplomatic communications in near-real time.

The "Purple break" opened a privileged window into Japanese diplomatic thinking at a critical moment. Deciphered Purple messages revealed how Tokyo explained its moves to its ambassadors, how it negotiated with Axis partners, and how it assessed American and Allied policy.

It provided strategic context that shaped high-level decisions on sanctions, negotiations, and war planning. It also marked a leap in American cryptologic capability: proof that U.S. analysts could reverse-engineer a sophisticated machine cipher by sheer intellectual effort.

Genevieve's contribution, largely unheralded at the time and long overshadowed by others' names, stands as a reminder that the breakthrough at the heart of one of the war's most crucial codebreaking successes came from a young woman at a shared desk, turning patterns in her head into a machine on a workbench.

By October 1943, she was assigned to Soviet communications and worked on what became Venona, again placing a woman at the center of high-stakes intelligence problems while remaining largely invisible outside classified circles.[2]

This is not "women helped." This is "one woman broke the code on a major enemy system." The work was essential, the secrecy was absolute, and the public credit was limited by design.

Decoding machine, right, built based on Grotjan's insight, being used to decode Japanese messages in WW II. By US Army photographer - Washington Post, October 21, 2017, Public Domain.

Bletchley Park and Breaking Enigma

Bletchley Park was never just a mansion full of lone male geniuses solving puzzles in silence. It was a dense, humming workplace in the English countryside where thousands of people—primarily young women—turned intercepted German signals into usable intelligence.

At the heart of this operation lay Enigma, the electro-mechanical cipher machine used by the German armed forces and other branches of the Nazi state. Its constantly changing letter substitutions were meant to make radio messages unreadable, but Bletchley's system turned that promise of secrecy into a vulnerability.

Women handled every stage of the codebreaking process. Some specialized in "cribbing" and traffic analysis—sorting and comparing intercepted messages to identify patterns and likely plaintext phrases. Others operated the bombes, large, noisy electromechanical devices that tested possible Enigma settings at high speed. Still others translated, indexed, and cross-checked the resulting decrypts, feeding a growing intelligence picture of German operations.

Daily life was closer to factory work than to spy fiction. Women stood for hours at the bombes, plugging in leads, resetting switches, recording candidate keys as the machines clattered through the night. In other sections, they sat at long tables, logging call signs, frequencies, and routines until they could recognize a German unit's "handwriting" by feel.

They learned to treat each fragment as part of a larger pattern: a call sign reappearing on a new frequency, a routine weather report embedded in a longer signal, or a convoy report that could be linked with others to map shipping lanes.

The work demanded precision, memory, and patience, and it wore on them, but it also offered a rare sense of direct connection to the war's course. A successful run on the bombes or a suddenly readable message could mean Allied ships were rerouted away from a U-boat wolf pack within hours.

The results of this labor, codenamed ULTRA, shaped the war in ways the women doing the work were rarely allowed to see. Enigma breaks gave the Allies insight into German submarine deployments in the Battle of the Atlantic, Luftwaffe plans during air campaigns, and, later, aspects of German responses to Allied deception before D-Day. Commanders saw concise intelligence summaries; the women at Bletchley saw countless tiny pieces that made those summaries possible.

Their contribution was not just raw effort but the creation of a new kind of information machine: layered teams, specialized tasks, and disciplined workflows designed to extract value from an overwhelming flow of enemy communications.

When the war ended, Bletchley Park closed almost as abruptly as it had begun. The Official Secrets Act bound its veterans from sharing information about the work they had performed, and many women went back to ordinary jobs or domestic life, carrying extraordinary experiences they could not discuss.

Their names rarely appeared in early histories of the war, which focused on a handful of male cryptanalysts and commanders. Only decades later, as documents were declassified and memoirs appeared, did the scale and character of their work become visible. It was another example of how crucial, skilled women's labor could be mission-critical yet remain invisible for a generation.

Silent Service: Women of Color Inside the Intelligence Machine

WWII home-front intelligence also carried segregation into secrecy. A unit of Black women cryptologists was formally established at Arlington Hall in early 1944, recruited and supervised by William Coffee, himself African American.[3] They contributed to the intelligence and monitoring apparatus even while separated from their white counterparts.

Black women held skilled positions, not just clerical roles, working as codebreakers, cryptologic clerks, and translators. Their unit focused heavily on commercial and financial traffic—screening private communications to detect whether U.S. companies were illegally trading with Nazi Germany or Japanese firms. Because their work was highly classified and shaped by Jim Crow record-keeping, only a few names are firmly documented.

Annie Briggs

One woman whose record survives is Annie Briggs, who led a production unit that processed and solved coded and enciphered messages, much of which was commercial and financial traffic used to detect prohibited trade with enemy nations. Briggs held a supervisory role, assigning work and managing output in a unit that fed directly into the larger U.S. signals intelligence system.[4]

Very little biographical information about her life beyond Arlington Hall survives in the declassified record. Still, her documented leadership position marks her as one of the few named Black women in wartime American codebreaking, and a concrete example of how women of color were trusted with complex, sensitive work while still confined to racially segregated spaces.

While home-front intelligence shows women managing secrets, the war industry allowed women to manage output—factories, shipyards, and production quotas that turned information and materials into victory.

The War Industry at Peak Scale

World War II made production a battlefield. Once the United States entered the war, victory depended on turning raw materials into ships, planes, tanks, ammunition, and supplies faster than the Axis could destroy them. That transformation required labor on a scale the prewar economy did not have—and the fastest available workforce was women.

Women moved into jobs that had been defined as male: aircraft assembly, shipbuilding support work, ordnance production, drafting rooms, inspection lines, and the dense administrative scaffolding that made mass production schedulable. The "Rosie the Riveter" figure did not appear by accident. The government actively promoted women as a patriotic workforce, with tools, lunch pails, uniforms, and factory identity folded into a new wartime image of womanhood.

Wartime industrial centers like the Kaiser shipyards in Richmond, California, grew into massive mixed-gender workforces under intense schedule pressure. The work was essential, but it was not gentle: long shifts, repetitive-motion demands, and injury risk were built into the pace of "maximum output."

Wartime production drew women across racial and ethnic lines into factories and defense workplaces, but it did so within unequal housing, job assignment, and promotion systems. The war expanded access to wages and skilled work for many women, while preserving barriers that shaped where women were hired, what jobs they were offered, and how quickly they could advance.

The state and industry recruited them, trained them, regulated their appearance and conduct, tracked their output, and then—when victory approached—began preparing the public for contraction. The war needed permanence.

The postwar economy wanted reversibility.

Daughters of Valor: Behind Enemy Lines

In occupied Europe, women were not on the margins of clandestine war; they were at its center.

Recruited into British Special Operations Executive (SOE), the American OSS, and local resistance groups, they learned to move through occupied streets as if nothing were wrong, carrying false papers, hidden radios, and messages that could cost them their lives if discovered. Officials often justified their deployment with gendered logic—arguing that women attracted less suspicion at checkpoints—but once in place, these women became organizers, couriers, wireless operators, and saboteurs in their own right.

Training stripped away any illusion that this was a "soft" assignment. Women selected for SOE or similar organizations went through the same paramilitary courses as men: weapons handling, demolition, hand-to-hand combat, clandestine communications, and the maintenance of convincing cover identities.

They learned how to jump from aircraft at night, how to set timers on explosives, how to send and receive coded wireless traffic under strict time limits to evade German direction-finding vans, and how to withstand interrogation if their story was challenged in a train compartment or at a roadblock.

On the ground, their work hinged on movement and memory. Many women served as couriers, bicycling or riding crowded trains across France, Belgium, the Netherlands, and beyond, carrying messages hidden in coat linings, hollowed-out books, or memorized to avoid carrying incriminating paper.

Others operated clandestine radios, encoding and transmitting nightly situation reports on German troop movements, supply depots, and morale to London, a task so dangerous that radio operators—male and female—had some of the shortest life expectancies in the field. Still others managed escape lines, guided downed Allied airmen over mountains or through occupied cities, arranged safe houses and food, and coordinated weapons and money drops for local resistance cells.

Survival depended as much on social intelligence as on weapons training. Women behind enemy lines had to read rooms and streets instantly, decide when to flirt, when to feign deference, when to be invisible, and when to project authority to get a collaborator or German officer to underestimate them or wave them through.

Capture remained a constant risk: dozens of female agents were arrested, tortured, deported to camps like Ravensbrück, or executed, paying with their lives for work that often remained secret for decades.

Their stories show that "training, operations, and survival" in occupied Europe were not three separate phases but an ongoing cycle—skills honed in Britain or neutral countries, tested on missions, and revised on the fly by women who learned, under occupation, how to stay alive and keep resisting at the same time.

Virginia Hall: The Limping Lady Who Became the Gestapo's Most Wanted

One such woman was Virginia Hall, the first woman to live behind enemy lines.

From Rejected Diplomat to SOE Recruit

Born in Baltimore in 1906, Virginia initially tried to enter the U.S. Foreign Service but was blocked—partly by gender bias and partly by a hunting accident in Turkey that cost her a lower leg, which she replaced with a wooden prosthesis.

When war came to Europe, she volunteered as an ambulance driver in France, where a British contact recognized her nerve, languages, and local knowledge and steered her toward the newly formed Special Operations Executive. SOE, created to "set Europe ablaze" through sabotage and resistance, needed people who could operate alone under pressure; despite her disability, Virginia fit the profile.

After SOE training in weapons, clandestine communications, and tradecraft, Virginia went into Vichy France in August 1941 as an undercover agent posing as a reporter. She became the first female SOE operative to take up long-term residence in France, tasked with building what became the "Heckler" network around Lyon.[5]

Over the next 15 months, she organized safe houses, arranged air drops of money and weapons, coordinated couriers, and helped downed Allied airmen and escaped prisoners move along clandestine escape lines, effectively turning herself into a one-woman logistics hub for the resistance in the region.

The Gestapo's "Most Dangerous" Spy

Her success made her a prime target. German security services and the Gestapo circulated wanted posters describing "the woman who limps," calling her "the most dangerous of all Allied spies." As German control tightened after the Allied landings in North Africa, her position became untenable. Warned that arrest was imminent, she escaped over the Pyrenees into Spain on her prosthetic leg, then returned to Britain, where she was decorated with the Order of the British Empire for her service.

Back Into France with the OSS

Virginia refused to stop. In 1944, she re-entered occupied France, this time as an Office of Strategic Services (OSS) operative and wireless officer in the "Saint" network, working in central France in the run-up to and aftermath of D-Day.

Operating with minimal support from other OSS agents, she trained Maquis guerrillas, coordinated arms drops, and directed sabotage against German rail lines and convoys, helping local forces in regions like Haute-Loire clear German troops ahead of advancing Allied armies.

Virginia Hall

Initially dismissed by her own government and physically disabled, she became pivotal to Allied operations behind enemy lines. She demonstrated that the core skills of clandestine work—planning, organizing, maintaining cover, and making rapid, risky decisions—were not only compatible with female agents but, in her case, exemplified at the highest level.

Her postwar move into the CIA's Special Activities Division extended that influence into the Cold War, making her not just a legendary SOE and OSS operator but a bridge between wartime resistance work and modern covert action.

Medical War at Scale: Nurses, Cadet Nurses, and the Chain of Evacuation

World War II expanded American military medicine into a global system, and women were essential to its functioning.

The Army Nurse Corps alone grew to more than 59,000 nurses during the war, serving not only in large base and general hospitals but increasingly close to combat through the Army's "chain of evacuation," which included field hospitals, evacuation hospitals, hospital trains and ships, and flight nursing on medical transport aircraft.

Nursing was no longer confined to rear areas; nurses worked under bombardment, in primitive conditions, and in theaters where disease and climate could be as dangerous as enemy fire.

The U.S. Cadet Nurse Corps trained and mobilized more than 100,000 women to staff civilian hospitals at home, freeing resources for overseas care and sustaining a wartime medical system that could not have survived on the existing labor supply.

In 1944, nurses in the Army and Navy Nurse Corps finally received commissions and full military benefits, a significant institutional acknowledgment that came only after years of service under military authority.

Nurses in the Crossfire: Prisoners of War

When Japan seized the Philippines in early 1942, 99 U.S. Army and Navy nurses were swept up in the collapse of American defenses. They became prisoners of war, yet they continued nursing throughout their captivity, improvising a hospital system inside prison camps.[6]

These women, later known as the "Angels of Bataan and Corregidor," had already worked under fire in field hospitals and tunnels during the siege, treating waves of wounded and malnourished soldiers with dwindling supplies. When U.S. forces surrendered, they followed their patients into captivity rather than accept evacuation or safety apart from them.

In the first months after surrender, many of the nurses were held at makeshift facilities and then transferred to the civilian internment camp at Santo Tomas in Manila, where they set up and ran a hospital within the camp. There, they cared for American and Allied civilians as well as military prisoners, confronting starvation, disease, and overcrowding with almost no drugs, dressings, or equipment. Beds were improvised from boards and straw; medicines were stretched, bartered for, or substituted with basic hygiene and careful nursing when pharmaceuticals ran out.

The nurses organized shifts, sanitation routines, and medical records, effectively creating a functioning infirmary inside a malnourished population.

Conditions deteriorated as the war dragged on. Food rations shrank, and diseases such as dysentery, beriberi, and tuberculosis spread. The nurses themselves grew thin, weak, and chronically ill. Even so, they stayed on their wards and schedules, often working in threadbare uniforms, reusing bandages, and making clinical decisions as best they could without doctors or supplies.

Their authority remained constrained by gender and rank—they were still women, still officers' subordinates, still prisoners—but in practice they became the backbone of camp health care, holding together a medical system that prevented even higher death rates among internees.

The nurses were held in captivity for nearly three years, until U.S. forces liberated the camps in 1945. Many emerged emaciated and ill, with long-term physical and psychological consequences, and for decades, their story received far less attention than combat narratives from the same theater.

Yet their experience in the Philippines shows what "service" could mean under extreme duress: continuing professional work without pay, freedom, or adequate tools; insisting that patients mattered even when the state that commissioned them had effectively vanished; and turning a prisoner-of-war camp into the last possible version of a hospital.

U.S. Army Nurses from Bataan and Corregidor, freed after three years imprisonment in Santo Tomas Interment Compound, climb into trucks as they leave Manila, Luzon, P.I., on their way home to the U.S. The nurses are wearing new uniforms given to them to replace their worn-out clothes. Public domain.

Unequal Representation Continues

Of the approximately 59,000 Army Nurse Corps nurses, only 479 African American nurses were accepted, and only after years of pressure and need.[7] Inclusion expanded in wartime, but on unequal terms, and often only when crisis made exclusion politically or operationally untenable. Japanese American women were admitted to the Army Nurse Corps starting in February 1943, but "only a handful" served there, and they generally did not receive overseas assignments. Chinese American women also served in the Army Nurse Corps and Navy Nurse Corps, but the numbers were not officially recorded.

First Lt. Elsie Chin Yuen Seetoo — Chinese American Nurse, U.S. Army Nurse Corps

Elsie Chin Yuen Seetoo entered the war not from an American base, but from the fault line between empires.

Born in Stockton, California, to Chinese immigrant parents, she returned with her family to China in 1931, trading Depression-era California for a country already under Japanese pressure. By December 1941, when Japan attacked Pearl Harbor, she was a working nurse in a world that turned to war overnight.

The shift from civilian to combat medicine came almost immediately. After the Japanese assault on Hong Kong, Seetoo moved into full wartime service, tending to the wounded in overwhelmed hospitals as shells and bombs remade the city around her.

When Hong Kong fell, staying meant almost certain capture. She escaped to Free China, disguised as a peasant, and journeyed more than 700 miles by boat and truck, and on foot—carrying her skills into shrinking spaces where Elsie's skills might still be allowed.

In Free China, she crossed the line from ally to American service member. She joined the U.S. Army Nurse Corps and became the first Chinese American nurse commissioned there, entering a corps that had only reluctantly begun to accept women of color.

Wearing a U.S. rank as a First Lieutenant, she served with the 14th Air Force's Air Service Command, moving through hospitals tied to American air operations in places such as Kunming, Chengdu, and later Shanghai.[8]

By U.S. Army Nurse Corps - U.S. Department of Veterans Affairs, news.VA.gov, Public Domain.

Her work sat at the junction of airpower and ground suffering: stabilizing aircrew and local patients alike so that the larger machine of war could keep turning

In 1946, Elsie returned to the United States and received the World War II Victory Medal and the Asiatic-Pacific Campaign Medal.

Her path—California to China, occupied Hong Kong to Free China, then into the U.S. Army Nurse Corps—captures how women of color could become indispensable inside American military medicine only by moving through multiple war zones and slipping past the racial and national boundaries that were supposed to keep them out.

Marcella Rose LeBeau (Lakota) — Army Nurse Corps

Marcella Rose LeBeau, a member of the Two Kettle Band of the Cheyenne River Sioux Tribe, served in the U.S. Army Nurse Corps during World War II, treating D-Day battle casualties.[9]

Marcella Rose LeBeau

She described the danger as immediate and physical: German attacks reaching the nurses' area, including a strafing incident and a buzz bomb striking near her quarters, killing personnel in a nearby tent.

She wasn't holding a weapon, but she was operating in a space where air attack and mass casualties made nursing a frontline condition. World War II demanded women's medical skills globally, and it exposed them to the war's lethal reach even when the institution categorized them as noncombatants.

Japanese American Women Nurses — Service Under a Contested Citizenship Climate

Japanese American women entered World War II nursing under a shadow that their white peers did not face.

In the months after Pearl Harbor, the federal government stripped West Coast Japanese American communities of homes, jobs, and freedom under Executive Order 9066, sending families to incarceration camps while branding them potential traitors.

Within that climate, Japanese American women who wanted to become nurses ran into explicit barriers: the Women's Army Auxiliary Corps refused them, and the Army Nurse Corps did not begin accepting Japanese American applicants until February 1943, more than a year into the war.

When the policy finally shifted, it did so for reasons that revealed the system's logic. Manpower and nurse shortages pushed the War Department and the Public Health Service to widen the pipeline, just as political pressure forced Congress to write a nondiscrimination clause into the 1943 Nurse Training Act that created the U.S. Cadet Nurse Corps. That clause opened the door for more than 400 Nisei women to train as cadet nurses and an estimated 200–350 Japanese American women to enter the Cadet Nurse Corps overall, including many recruited directly out of incarceration camps with the promise of tuition and a way out.[10]

A much smaller number—described in contemporary accounts as "only a handful"—qualified for and joined the Army Nurse Corps itself, and they were generally kept in stateside posts rather than being sent overseas.

For the women who took these paths, service meant moving through institutions that still did not fully want them. Nursing schools participating in the Cadet Nurse Corps could legally enroll Nisei students. Still, only about 70 of more than a thousand schools opened their doors, citing fears that patients and staff would not trust Japanese American nurses. Those who did get in underwent the same accelerated 30-month training and signed the same wartime service commitments as their white peers, while also enduring FBI checks, racist harassment, and the knowledge that parents or siblings remained behind barbed wire.

Seen from the state's side, these nurses embodied a stark contradiction. Policy makers constructed Japanese Americans as a suspect racial category, removed them en masse from the Pacific Coast, and then, once shortages and political scrutiny intensified, selectively extracted their daughters for military and quasi-military nursing roles.

Seen from the women's side, enlistment offered a narrow kind of agency: a chance to leave the camps, to prove loyalty in visible form, to gain education and wages, and to transform a stigmatized identity into professional service.

The result was a generation of Japanese American nurses who practiced care despite a system that had first marked them as dangerous.

Aiko "Grace" Obata

Aiko "Grace" Obata Amemiya's war began with a train ride behind barbed wire.

A young Japanese American nursing student from Northern California, she watched her ordinary life change when her family was ordered to a series of detention centers after Pearl Harbor. Official notices and military police treated them as a "problem population" to be removed from the coast, a security risk that had to be enclosed and monitored rather than educated or employed.

Inside camp, however, the logic shifted. Running short on qualified nurses, recruiters came into some camps with brochures and promises: join the Cadet Nurse Corps, leave the barracks for a nursing school, and serve where the country needed you most.

Aiko took that offer. Selected as a cadet nurse, she left Gila River in Arizona for training at a mainstream hospital nursing school, stepping from incarceration into a federally funded, patriotic program.

Her days turned into a blur of clinical rotations, lectures, and night shifts on crowded wartime wards, treating soldiers, industrial workers, and civilians under the same national emergency that had justified her family's confinement. She wore the Cadet Nurse Corps gray uniform and patch, symbols of inclusion in a national nursing sisterhood that posters depicted as the equal of any fighting branch.

The dissonance never entirely disappeared. On paper, she was a federal trainee in an elite program created to save the home-front medical system from collapse; on paper, her parents and siblings were "evacuees" confined in a relocation center for the duration. Her paychecks and training orders carried the authority of the same government that had taken her family's home.

When the war ended, she emerged as a trained nurse with a federally recognized credential and a profession that would sustain her in peacetime—while her wartime "loyalty" record coexisted with camp photographs and exclusion orders.

The Rollback: Victory, Demobilization, and the Re-Shrinking Definition of "Service" (Again)

The end of the war triggered a familiar institutional reflex: contraction. As millions of men returned from overseas, government and employers moved quickly to "reconvert" the economy and reassert prewar norms about who should hold jobs and authority.

The pattern was immediate: women were demobilized from wartime work—especially in "men's jobs"—to make room for returning servicemen. "Temporary" became the controlling word: women were celebrated as essential during the emergency and treated as expendable once the emergency passed.

This rollback applied to:

Industry: women who had built planes, welded ships, and held production lines together were pushed out through layoffs, seniority rules rewritten around veteran preference, and social pressure framed as patriotic "normalcy."

Military service: women's units were reduced sharply after V-J Day, wartime recruitment pipelines closed, and women's presence in uniform was narrowed again.

Memory: wartime propaganda that had portrayed women as the answer to labor shortage was replaced by a cultural campaign for domestic restoration, turning the war's workforce into a symbol rather than a precedent.

What makes WWII different from earlier wars is not that the rollback occurred, but that it happened after the country had already built an industrial, administrative, and intelligence architecture that proved women could function at scale inside national systems. In other words, WWII did not merely show women's capabilities. It showed institutional dependence—and then exposed how quickly institutions tried to forget it when dependence was no longer urgent.

The rollback was real, but it was not complete. The Cold War would soon force the United States back into permanent readiness—meaning women's wartime "exceptions" would become recurring necessities, and the fight for status would continue inside a system that had already learned it could not operate without them.

[1] "Genevieve Grotjan Feinstein," National Security Agency; "Red and Purple," NSA Cryptologic History Series.
[2] "Genevieve Grotjan Feinstein," National Security Agency
[3] "William Coffee," NSA Cryptologic Hall of Honor; "The Secret Journey of the NSA's First African-American Cryptologists."
[4] "The Black Women Code Breakers of Arlington Hall Station," Arlington Magazine; "The Invisible Cryptologists: African-Americans, WWII to 1956," National Security Agency.
[5] Virginia Hall," The National Archives (UK); "Virginia Hall—SOE Agent to CIA Pioneer," History Guild.
[6] "Military Nurses in the Philippines," National Park Service; "Nurse POWs: Angels of Bataan and Corregidor," The National WWII Museum.
[7] "African American Army Nurses in World War II," National Park Service; The Army Nurse Corps, U.S. Army Center of Military History.
[8] "Elsie Chin Yuen Seetoo," Veterans Legacy Program, U.S. Department of Veterans Affairs.
[9] "Marcella (Ryan) LeBeau," Army Nurse Corps, World War II; The Color of Freedom exhibit, Military Women's Memorial; "Dakota Images: Marcella LeBeau," South Dakota History 52, no. 2 (2022).
[10] "Cadet Nurse Corps," National Park Service; "Japanese American Women in Service," National Park Service.

Part IV — Women During Wartime in Korea, Vietnam and The Cold War: Service and Sacrifice

Chapter 6 — Korea and Permanent Readiness

"Our orders said noncombatant. The incoming artillery said otherwise."

— U.S. Army Nurse

THE KOREAN WAR (1950–1953) was the moment the United States learned how to fight a "limited" war with a permanent war machine.

The Korean War (1950–1953) began when North Korea invaded South Korea on June 25, 1950, quickly becoming a UN-led war dominated by fast-moving front lines, air power, and high-stakes decisions under nuclear-era pressure. What began as a local struggle on the Korean Peninsula quickly hardened into the first large confrontation of the Cold War, pulling U.S. and United Nations forces into a protracted ground and air campaign against North Korean and, soon, Chinese troops.

While the conflict in Korea was never as explosively controversial as Vietnam, it was uneasy and unpopular in a quieter way, both while it was being fought and in how it was remembered.

Early on, many Americans accepted intervention as part of a wider Cold War struggle—framed as defending South Korea and containing communism under the new United Nations system—but support was thin and highly sensitive to losses and setbacks, Polling from the time shows that within months of the 1950 invasion, large portions of the public were already calling the war a "mistake," with opinion swinging back and forth as peace talks stalled and casualty lists grew.

Several features made the war feel frustrating and, to many, not worth the cost. It was not declared as a formal war by Congress but was sold as a "police action" under UN authority, leaving some citizens feeling the country had slid into conflict without a clear decision or end state.

The fighting also quickly bogged down into a bloody stalemate near the 38th parallel, so that battles costing thousands of lives seemed to shift the front only marginally, feeding a sense of endless sacrifice without visible progress. Serving in an unpopular war meant that those in uniform often carried two burdens at once: the dangers and demands of military service, and the knowledge that many people at home opposed the very war they were helping to sustain.

Unlike World War II, there was no call for total national mobilization; instead, the country fought while factories, schools, and suburbs stayed open, relying on a standing military and an already-built global support apparatus.

That structure changed the rhythm of war. Korea ran on continuous readiness: large active-duty forces, long supply lines, and medical and evacuation systems that stayed in motion without the promise of a clear "demobilization" at the end.

The old pattern—build a giant wartime machine and then tear it down in peacetime—gave way to something closer to a permanent mobilization in the background. Bases, hospitals, and command staffs created for World War II did not disappear; they were reactivated and extended, stitched into a Cold War network that assumed more crises would follow.

For women, this continuity mattered more than the official headlines. The nursing services, administrative corps, communications units, and intelligence offices assembled during World War II were not reinvented for Korea; they were reopened, often in the same forms, with the same job descriptions and the same ceilings on rank and authority.

Women who had worn uniforms in the 1940s—or followed those paths just after—now found that the "temporary" wartime opportunities had been quietly built into the architecture of a new, peacetime-and-war military.

Korea did not introduce women to conflict: it tested whether their labor would finally be treated as permanent rather than provisional.

New World Order

When World War II ended, only about 22,000 women were still in U.S. uniform, remnants of what many assumed had been a temporary wartime experiment. At the start of the Korean War, the United States once again called on women to staff hospitals, manage records, run communications, and perform technical work that it now recognized as essential.

By the time the Korean War was underway, the number of women in uniform had grown to roughly 120,000 on active duty, with about one-third of them working in health care.

Women entered this new war through the branches created or expanded in World War II: the Women's Army Corps (WAC), Women in the Air Force (WAF), the Navy's WAVES, and the Women Marines.

On paper, these were auxiliary or parallel structures; in practice, they supplied the nurses, technicians, clerks, communications staff, and specialists who kept the system running. Many volunteered specifically as nurses or medical staff, knowing that Korea's front lines and evacuation chains would need more hands than the peacetime corps could supply.

For medical personnel, Korea meant working wherever wounded bodies moved. Army nurses staffed Mobile Army Surgical Hospitals—MASH units—close to the fighting, stabilizing casualties in canvas operating rooms before sending them farther back. Others served on hospital ships offshore, in MEDEVAC aircraft that shuttled patients out of the war zone, and in larger hospitals in Japan, Hawaii, and the continental United States that received the wounded from Korea for longer-term care.

Together, they formed a continuous chain of treatment stretching from muddy aid stations to polished stateside wards, showing that by the early 1950s, women's military labor was no longer a brief wartime exception, but part of how the United States fought and recovered from war.

Korea: Blurred Lines, MASH Units and Combat

The Korean War placed American military medicine closer to combat than at any previous point, and women, primarily nurses, were integral to that shift.

The introduction of Mobile Army Surgical Hospitals (MASH) fundamentally changed battlefield care. Designed to be positioned near the front lines, MASH units prioritized speed: rapid surgery, stabilization, and evacuation rather than prolonged recovery. The goal was survival through immediacy, and that goal depended on nurses who could function under fire, exhaustion, and a constant flow of casualties.

For Army nurses, Korea was not a repeat of World War II— it was more concentrated, more exposed, and less buffered by scale. MASH units operated in tents and rudimentary structures, often within range of artillery and small-arms fire. Nurses worked long, uninterrupted shifts treating traumatic injuries—shrapnel wounds, gunshot wounds, burns, and frostbite—while managing shock and blood loss with limited resources.

The proximity to combat collapsed the remaining fiction that nursing was "rear-area" service. In Korea, care was delivered where the fighting was still audible.

Korea's terrain and climate added another layer of pressure. In winter, trucks and stretchers arrived with soldiers stiff from cold as well as from injury, and nurses had to treat frostbite, hypothermia, and respiratory complications alongside battlefield wounds. In the summer heat and monsoon rains, infection became a constant threat; dressings had to be changed more often, wounds had to be observed for redness and swelling, and exhausted staff pushed themselves to maintain hygiene in mud-spattered facilities.

By the time the war began in 1950, the United States no longer disbanded its medical corps between conflicts. Women were no longer temporary substitutes for absent men; they were part of a standing military system. Yet permanence did not equal parity. Nurses held commissions, adhered to military discipline, and faced combat-adjacent danger, yet they remained officially classified as noncombatants and excluded from decision-making authority commensurate with their responsibilities.

Korea exposed the contradiction sharply: women were close enough to die, but not close enough to be counted on paper as fighters.

Race remained embedded in this system. Black nurses served in Korea following President Truman's 1948 executive order desegregating the armed forces, yet integration was uneven and often resisted in practice. Women of color were no longer excluded outright, but equality was incomplete and situational, shaped by unit culture and command enforcement rather than policy alone.

MASH nursing also marks a cultural turning point. Survival rates improved dramatically because of forward surgical care, and nurses were central to that success. The system worked because women were already trained, already commissioned, already embedded. Korea proved that women's military medical labor was not an emergency adaptation—it was a permanent requirement of modern war.

Evelyn Decker – 8055th MASH

Evelyn Decker entered the Army Nurse Corps at a hinge moment, when the rules had changed, but the culture hadn't.

Although Order 9981 had formally ordered the desegregation of the armed forces, Black service members in 1950 still encountered segregated facilities, unequal assignments, and commanding officers who treated integration as optional.

Against this backdrop, Evelyn stepped into her role as an African American nurse, wearing a U.S. uniform in a system still deciding whether it truly meant to see her as an equal professional or merely as proof of compliance on paper.

Evelyn's Dream

Evelyn Decker dreamed of being a doctor. It was an ambition shaped early and abandoned just as quickly, undone by circumstance rather than ability. Her father died young, leaving her mother to raise four daughters on her own, and medical school was simply out of reach.

In 1936, she chose the practical path that remained, enrolling in nursing school in Harlem. Eight years later, with the world at war and the United States fully engaged, she carried that training into uniform, joining the U.S. Army in 1944 as World War II reached its most punishing years. Because Evelyn was black and segregation split the Army of 1944, she could work only in black hospitals, treating only black soldiers. She recalled being forced to work in hospital laundry rooms, and once was pulled over and jailed while stationed in Maryland because a white officer couldn't believe a black woman was legally wearing a military uniform.

8055th MASH Unit

When Evelyn deployed to Korea, she was one of only a handful of black nurses. She joined the 8055th MASH unit, a mobile army surgical hospital (MASH) and evacuation hospital established near the front.[1]

Casualties arrived by jeep or ambulance and, increasingly, by helicopter—men pulled directly from ridgelines and rice paddies into canvas operating rooms and prefabricated huts. Her work began at that threshold. She helped triage the wounded, establish IV lines, administer morphine and plasma, and prepare patients for emergency surgery within minutes of arrival.

Inside the MASH tents and evacuation hospitals, the pace rarely slowed. Surgeons could operate only if nurses like Evelyn kept the flow organized: lining up cases by urgency, monitoring anesthesia, watching for signs of shock, and managing postoperative care in crowded recovery wards.

For Evelyn and her colleagues, the casualty stream seemed endless: battles like Pusan, Inchon, Chosin, and the back-and-forth fighting near the 38th parallel all translated into nights when cots lined every available corner and sleep came in snatches, if at all.

She confronted catastrophic trauma as routine—shrapnel wounds, burns, amputations, and chest and abdominal injuries from artillery and small-arms fire—all under conditions that bore little resemblance to stateside hospitals. Power could flicker; supplies did not always arrive on time; and sterility was an aspiration rather than a guarantee. Nursing became both technical and improvisational, a constant exercise in doing as much as possible with the equipment and time at hand.

Evelyn Decker

Layered on top of this was the unfinished project of integration. In principle, she wore the same insignia and held the same commission as white Army nurses. In practice, she navigated a world where ward assignments, living quarters, promotions, and informal social life could still be shaped by race—sometimes subtly, sometimes not.

She had to prove clinical competence under the same unforgiving conditions as any nurse, while also navigating mess halls, officers' clubs, and chain-of-command dynamics that did not always welcome her. Her service, then, was not just a test of skill and stamina at the edge of the battlefield; it was a test case for whether the desegregated Army would allow a Black woman officer to exercise that skill and authority without being pushed back into the margins.

Her work inside MASH and evacuation hospitals makes clear that desegregation was not an abstract policy debate. It played out in triage tents, operating rooms, and recovery wards, where an African American nurse's decisions could mean the difference between life and death for soldiers who, only a few years earlier, might never have expected to see a Black woman in that role at all.

Colonel Ruby Bradley: From POW Survivor to Korean War Hero

Colonel Ruby Bradley had already survived thirty-seven months in a Japanese prisoner-of-war camp during World War II when she volunteered to serve in Korea in 1950, determined to use her hard-won medical expertise to save lives on yet another battlefield.[2] At fifty-three years old, she would become one of the most decorated women in American military history, performing surgery in freezing

MASH units and evacuating wounded soldiers under enemy fire during one of the war's most brutal winters.

Born in 1907 in rural West Virginia, Ruby became a nurse in 1933 and joined the Army Nurse Corps the following year, long before women in uniform were visible in public life. By 1941, she was serving in the Philippines as an Army nurse at Camp John Hay on Luzon when Japan attacked Pearl Harbor and, soon after, overran U.S. positions in the islands.

Captured by Japanese forces, she spent 37 months as a prisoner of war in camps, including Santo Tomas in Manila. Inside those barbed-wire worlds, she and other Army nurses set up makeshift dispensaries and operating rooms, smuggling in morphine, surgical tools, and bandages as their uniforms grew loose from hunger. Over three years, she assisted in roughly 230 major operations. She helped deliver 13 babies, earning from fellow prisoners the nickname "Angel in Fatigues" for her habit of going without food so children and the most vulnerable adults could eat.[3]

Liberation in February 1945 brought her out of captivity, but not out of the Army; after recuperation, she returned to stateside posts and chose to remain in uniform as the world shifted into the Cold War.

When North Korea invaded the South in June 1950, Ruby was in her early forties and a veteran of one brutal war, yet she went back overseas. She became Chief Nurse of the 171st Evacuation Hospital. This large facility received patients from forward MASH units and smaller clearing stations as the front line surged up and down the peninsula. The 171st leapfrogged with the fighting—Daegu in the south, then forward to Pyongyang after the Inchon landings, then back again as Chinese forces poured into the war.

In tent wards and hastily converted buildings, Ruby saw an endless stream of wounded. She and her team of nurses stabilized patients recovering from emergency surgery, managed blood transfusions and antibiotics, and tried to prevent shock and infection in conditions where cold, mud, and overcrowding were constant enemies.

Her most famous moment in Korea came in November 1950, when a massive Chinese counteroffensive forced U.S. forces to evacuate Pyongyang. As roughly 100,000 Chinese troops closed in, orders came down for medical staff to pull out. Ruby refused to leave until every patient and staff member from the 171st had been loaded onto planes, and only when the last stretcher was aboard did she climb up the ramp herself.[4]

She reached safety just as the ambulance that had brought her to the airfield exploded under enemy shellfire, a scene she later recalled with characteristic understatement: "You got to get out in a hurry when you have somebody behind you with a gun."

After Pyongyang, she again advanced in responsibility. In 1951, she became Assistant Nursing Consultant and then Chief Nurse of the Eighth Army's Medical Section, overseeing roughly 500 Army nurses throughout Korea and shaping how the entire theater's nursing service was staffed and run. She remained in Korea until shortly before the 1953 armistice and received a full-dress honor guard upon her departure—reportedly the first woman in Army history to receive such a send-off.

By the time she retired in 1963 as a colonel, she had earned 34 medals and citations, including two Legions of Merit, two Bronze Stars, and the Florence Nightingale Medal. She was widely regarded as one of the most decorated women in U.S. Army history.

Women in the Air

The Korean War was the first time the new U.S. Air Force had to fight a sustained war on its own, as a separate branch rather than an offshoot of the Army.

Created in 1947, the service went to war in 1950, still debating its doctrine, building its personnel system, and establishing a global network of bases to support jet aircraft, bombers, and round-the-clock operations.

Women arrived in this unsettled institution under a law that both recognized and constrained them. The Women's Armed Services Integration Act of June 12, 1948, finally granted women permanent status in the regular forces—but it also capped their numbers at 2 percent of overall strength and framed their roles as strictly limited support, not as peers to male aircrew and combat officers.

Those limits determined where women could go when fighting broke out on the Korean Peninsula. Policy drew a hard line around the combat zone: during the war, Air Force flight nurses were the only women in the service permitted to operate in or over Korea itself. Strapped into litters and jump seats on transport aircraft, they moved the wounded from rough airstrips and forward fields to better-equipped facilities, providing in-flight care in an environment the Air Force defined as medical support yet that exposed them to many of the same risks as the men they were evacuating. Every other woman in Air Force blue was kept behind that line.

Behind it, however, women's work became part of the machinery that made the air war possible. The rest of the Women in the Air Force (WAF) served at rear-area bases in Japan, in roles that did not drop bombs but helped determine whether bombs could be dropped at all.

WAF air traffic controllers managed crowded runways and air corridors, deciding when and how aircraft took off and landed. Weather observers gathered and interpreted data that could scrub missions or green-light strikes. Radar operators and photo interpreters sifted signals and images, tracing enemy movements, mapping targets, and feeding commanders the information they needed to plan sorties and assess damage. On paper, these were "noncombat" billets; in practice, they were intelligence-adjacent and information-critical positions that shaped every phase of air operations.

The Korean War also accelerated a medical revolution that had been building since World War II: aeromedical evacuation. In Korea, speed meant survival. Wounded soldiers were moved from aid stations and surgical hospitals into aircraft—often before they were stable by peacetime standards—because rapid transport to higher-level care could be the difference between life and death. That system worked only if the aircraft functioned as a flying ward. That responsibility fell heavily on flight nurses, who monitored shock, bleeding, pain, and post-operative instability in tight spaces, at altitude, and with limited equipment. The "front" did not end at the airstrip; it continued in the cabin.

By June 1953, as the war ground toward armistice, the numbers told their own story. WAF strength in Japan peaked at roughly 600 women, while total WAF strength worldwide climbed to about 12,800.[5] Those figures show an Air Force that had learned to rely on women's labor across its global network, expanding the scale and technical complexity of their work even as it kept most of them physically outside the designated combat zone.

The service that prided itself on mobility and reach thus carried forward a familiar contradiction: women's skills were now integral to how it fought, yet policy still treated their presence at the heart of danger as the exception, not the rule.

Janice Feagin Britton —Flight Nurse, 801st Medical Air Evacuation Squadron

Janice Feagin Britton's war ran along the air routes between Japan and the Korean Peninsula, in aircraft that doubled as flying hospital wards.

Born in 1921 in Montgomery, Alabama, she trained as a nurse at Vanderbilt University, graduating in 1944 as World War II still raged. The following year, she joined the U.S. Army Air Corps and was assigned to the 801st Medical Air

Evacuation Squadron, beginning a career in which her "hospital" would often be the cabin of a transport plane.[6]

When the Air Force became an independent service in 1947, Britton transferred to the new branch and continued as a flight nurse. From September 1950 to June 1951, as the Korean War intensified, she was among the 36 flight nurses assigned to the 801st, based in western Japan.

Their job was to shuttle into and out of Korea, picking up wounded soldiers at airstrips near the front and transporting them to better-equipped hospitals in Japan, then farther on if needed. In an oral history, she described the aircraft they used—the C-54 Skymaster—as the workhorse of the system: a four-engine transport whose interior could be fitted with tiers of litters, transforming its fuselage into what she called a "flying ward."

Inside that metal tube, Janice's work was technical, physical, and constant. She and the small aeromedical teams she led administered oxygen, adjusted splints, and managed pain for dozens of patients at a time, all while dealing with vibration, engine noise, and the shifting air pressure and temperature at altitude.

The C-54's layout determined what she could do: narrow aisles, stacked litters, and limited space for equipment meant that every move had to be planned, every piece of gear secured against turbulence.

She was often the highest-ranking and most medically trained person on board, responsible for triaging who needed attention first and for deciding when a patient was too unstable to fly and had to be left for later evacuation.

Her missions followed the war's rhythm. In the early months, she flew out of Japan into a fluid, dangerous theater: Pusan in the south, then fields nearer the 38th parallel, then farther north and back again as front lines surged with the Inchon landing and Chinese intervention.

Each leg meant loading litters as fast as the ground crews could bring them, taking off under blackout conditions, and then spending hours in the air moving from patient to patient, listening through the roar of the engines for changes in breathing or pain that signaled trouble.

In interviews, Janice emphasized the practicalities rather than the drama: the weight of oxygen bottles, the challenge of keeping IVs running in cold cabins, and the need to stay calm for patients who had never flown before and now found themselves strapped to a stretcher thousands of feet in the air.

By the time she left the Air Force in the early 1950s, Britton had reached the rank of captain and had built a career that literally spanned continents—later working as a nurse in Europe and serving in the Peace Corps in Zambia, continuing the pattern of taking her skills wherever they were most needed.

Janice's post-war life included two marriages, and in later years, she was part of a blended family with several stepchildren. Her public legacy centered on flight nursing, international service, and community work rather than on marriage and motherhood – the traditional roles for the era.

The Cold War Begins

The early Cold War opened a new kind of conflict: one in which the most critical moves often occurred in briefing rooms, embassies, and listening posts rather than on traditional battlefields.

The United States and the Soviet Union emerged from World War II as rival superpowers with nuclear weapons, global alliances, and a growing fear that the next misstep could trigger a war no one could survive. Rather than declaring war and mobilizing entire societies, both sides relied on proxies, covert operations, and constant surveillance—seeking advantages without crossing the line into open world war.

In this environment, governments poured resources into intelligence. Work that began in World War II, like reading cables, breaking codes, analyzing aerial photographs, and cultivating informants, became strategic tools on par with tanks and artillery. In Korea, most of the vital work happened in rooms full of radios, maps, and glowing radar screens.

Decisions about where to move troops or whether to escalate a crisis increasingly depended on what analysts and codebreakers could discern in the opponent's plans. For women, this shift mattered: it opened more roles in communications, analysis, and technical work, even though many of those jobs remained classified and undervalued.

Korea was the first significant test of this new order. Officially, it was a limited war on a single peninsula; in reality, it was also a Cold War laboratory where intelligence failures and successes shaped everything from the initial surprise of the North Korean invasion to later misjudgments about Chinese intentions.

The same system that had come to rely on women's labor during World War II now drew them into a different front line—operating radios and radars, decoding messages, staffing operations centers, and nursing in mobile hospitals—while still insisting that the "real" war was elsewhere, at the point of the gun.

For the Air Force, this is where most women served. They were kept at bases in Japan and held jobs that quietly shaped every air mission: running radar sets that tracked aircraft, interpreting reconnaissance photos to spot enemy movements and supply dumps, typing and routing classified reports, and working in operations centers that stitched all that information together. In practice, they sat close to the nerve center of the air war, even if official language still called their roles "support."

In that setting, intelligence was not an abstract term; it was a daily survival tool. Crews needed to know where enemy fighters were flying, where anti-aircraft guns had moved, and which roads and rail lines were feeding the front.

Analysts and operators pulled that picture together from three main streams. Signals and communications work (SIGINT/COMINT) meant listening for, recording, and trying to understand enemy radio traffic—who was talking, on what frequency, and about what. Imagery work (IMINT) meant studying aerial photos to identify new trenches, camouflaged positions, bridges, or trains, then briefing pilots on what to expect. Human reporting (HUMINT) added what local sources, prisoners, or friendly forces on the ground were observing.

Behind those acronyms were long shifts and repetitive tasks. People doing SIGINT and COMINT had to catch transmissions in real time, log call signs, help with basic translation or coding, and pass promising material to cryptologic specialists. The Korean War came after a major post–World War II drawdown, so the United States had to scramble to expand its code and communications analysis again, reopening and enlarging units that had gone quiet.

Women in those offices helped rebuild that capacity: they operated interception gear, handled traffic logs, and worked in the clerical and analytical backrooms that made higher-level codebreaking possible.

For WAF personnel in Japan, this meant living with a strange mix of distance and immediacy. Their jobs did not involve firing weapons, yet the information they processed determined where those weapons were used, how safely crews could fly, and how well commanders understood the enemy's actions.

Yvonne C. Pateman — WAF, the "China Watcher"

Yvonne C. Pateman's career sat at the intersection between the old, ground-focused Army Air Forces and the new Cold War Air Force that fought with information as much as with bombs. In a 1951 photograph, she appears not behind a typewriter but at the front of a briefing room, uniform crisp, pointer in hand, explaining to a room of pilots headed toward the Korean theater the Chinese military and political leaders. Her commanding officer called her his "China watcher," a joking title that precisely captured how central her work was: she was there to help aircrew understand not just where they were flying, but whose decisions and chains of command lay behind the targets on their maps.[7]

Yvonne's job was part of the Air Force's expanding intelligence system. As an intelligence officer, she would have been responsible for assembling briefing materials that drew on multiple sources: diplomatic reporting on Chinese leadership, military assessments of the Chinese People's Volunteer Forces, and current information on how Chinese commanders were coordinating with North Korean units.

In practical terms, this meant turning dense cables, situation reports, and reference manuals into something pilots could absorb quickly before a mission—charts of key leaders and their roles, maps showing where certain commanders operated, notes on how Chinese patterns of behavior might affect anti-aircraft defenses or the likelihood of rapid counterattacks.

Yvonne's presence in that room also shows how women's roles were shifting. A few years earlier, women around aircraft were expected to be clerks, drivers, or ferry pilots; now, a woman in uniform was the one with the map and the answers, giving the final word before men took off into hostile airspace.

The era's limits still constrained her job—she could brief combat missions but not fly them—but within those limits she occupied an essential Cold War position: the specialist whose understanding of an adversary's leadership, politics, and patterns of behavior could help turn raw firepower into something more precise and, for the crews listening to her, more survivable.

Lives Lost

Twenty American women lost their lives in the Korean War. Some were in uniform; others were war correspondents who accompanied male troops to the front lines to cover combat; several were civilian women.

Wilma Ledbetter

On a foggy evening in August 1950, the hospital ship USS Benevolence lay just off San Francisco, four miles west of the Golden Gate. It had finished sea trials and was preparing to return to service for a new war.

Out of the mist came the commercial freighter Mary Luckenbach, its bow cutting across the fog-shrouded shipping lanes. The collision tore into the Benevolence's side with little warning for those below decks.

Less than an hour later, the ship was gone. The Benevolence rolled and capsized, leaving only a slice of hull and a great red cross visible above the waterline as the rest disappeared beneath the surface

In the freezing Pacific, hundreds of men and women fought to stay afloat in oil-slicked swells, clinging to debris or life rafts while rescue craft tried to find them in the fog. Twenty-three people from the ship died that night; many more were pulled from the water on the edge of hypothermia.

Wilma Ledbetter

Among those thrown overboard were fifteen Navy nurses. They had been preparing to staff a hospital ship bound to support the Korean War; now they were patients of the sea themselves, battling cold and exhaustion alongside the rest of the crew. Fourteen of the nurses were eventually rescued.

One, Lieutenant Wilma Ledbetter, did not make it out alive, becoming an early reminder that even far from enemy fire, the work of caring for the wounded carried its own risks and its own dead.[8]

Post War Legacy

Korea left women with more rank, more permanence, and more medals than earlier wars—but still less visibility and symbolic recognition than their contributions warranted. It also locked in a Cold War pattern: a standing military that quietly depended on women while insisting, in law and monument, that war remained a male domain.

Medals and recognition after Korea

World War II nurses and women's corps members had already opened the door to formal awards, collecting more than 1,600 medals, citations, and commendations between them.

Korea continued that pattern on a smaller scale. Nurses and other women in Korea received Bronze Stars, Air Medals, and campaign ribbons, and their service counted toward the seniority that would later lift women like Anna Mae Hays—who served as a chief nurse in Korea—to become the Army's first female brigadier general in 1970, a promotion she explicitly framed as honoring "Army nurses throughout the world since 1901."

Yet compared to World War II, recognition remained thin and scattered. There were no large, Korea-specific medal programs for women as a group, and most decorations went to individuals without shifting the overall narrative of the war.

The "Forgotten War" label hurt them twice: first by overshadowing the conflict itself and second by burying women's roles even deeper within a story already treated as marginal. The Korean War Memorial in Washington, D.C., for example, features only male statues; women appear, if at all, as small etched figures in the background, reinforcing the sense that their work was secondary despite the 120,000 women on active duty and the one-third who were healthcare providers.

A Permanent Apparatus, but Provisional Status

Institutionally, Korea marked the point where women's presence stopped being a temporary wartime fix and became part of the permanent military apparatus. At the same time, the rules retained their explicit status as limited.

The Integration Act of 1948 capped women at 2 percent of each branch, barred them from combat roles, and restricted how high they could rise in rank and command. Korea, therefore, became a test run for a Cold War pattern: women used continuously, in essential roles, inside a military that planned for long-term global commitments—but still treated as a small, tightly bound minority whose careers could be cut short by pregnancy or policy changes.

Rigid Societal Expectations of Women

In the 1950s, as society became increasingly rigid about acceptable women's roles, the U.S. government established rules that quietly pushed many women out of the military the moment they became mothers—or even just wives. In fact, to wear the uniform, they were often expected to have no family at all.

Executive Order 10240

In 1951, President Truman signed an order that gave the services permission to force a woman out if she was, in almost any way, a parent. Under this order, a woman could be separated from service if she:

- had a child by birth or adoption.
- had custody of a child.
- was a stepmother, and the stepchild lived in her home for over a certain amount of time.
- became pregnant.
- gave birth to a living child while she was still serving.

In other words, once a woman moved from "single, childless service member" to "mother" or even "responsible for someone else's child," the military could treat that as grounds for ending her career. Therein lies the underlying and constant tension for women: they were allowed to serve, but only as long as their bodies and home lives stayed within the limits the institution set.

Later historians point directly to this order as the government's answer to a "new problem": what to do about pregnancy now that women were part of the regular armed forces, not just temporary wartime helpers. Instead of building systems to support military mothers, the solution was to remove them.

Marriage Rules: Always Moving Goalposts

Marriage was handled primarily by each service's internal rules, and those rules shifted depending on manpower needs. The official Women's Army Corps (WAC) history notes that:

- Women could be discharged when they married, under certain conditions, and those rules could be loosened during wartime or tightened again in peace.
- Pregnancy had long been an automatic reason for discharge, and once a pregnancy was confirmed, the process moved quickly.

Heading into Vietnam

As the United States moved deeper into the Cold War and toward Vietnam, Korea left three main legacies for women in uniform:

Proof of Indispensability

The success of MASH medicine, aeromedical evacuation, and large rear-area hospital systems depended on trained nurses and medics, many of them women, and the Air Force and Army carried those models straight into Vietnam.

Normalization without Full Equality

By the 1960s, it was no longer remarkable to see women in uniform at major bases, in hospitals, or in certain technical jobs; what remained controversial was letting them command mixed units, fly combat aircraft, or receive high-profile valor awards.

A Template for "Limited" Wars

Korea showed how the U.S. could fight intense, prolonged conflicts with a professional force and a fixed support apparatus rather than total national mobilization—and women were built into that apparatus from the start.

Korea was not a dramatic breakthrough for women, but more of a long transitional arc to service: women left the war with more institutional footholds than in 1945, but they were still largely absent from the public story and the memorial landscape.

The system had finally accepted their labor as permanent. However, it would take Vietnam and the later all-volunteer era to begin seriously questioning why their authority and recognition were still treated as temporary.

[1] Charles B. Rangel, "Recognizing the Contributions of Captain Evelyn Decker," Congressional Record, 110th Cong., 2nd sess., June 23, 2008, E1325–E1326.
[2] "Ruby Bradley," e-WV: The West Virginia Encyclopedia; "Army Veteran Ruby Bradley," U.S. Department of Veterans Affairs.
[3] "Ruby Bradley, 94; Army Nurse Was 'Angel in Fatigues' for POWs," Los Angeles Times, June 2, 2002.
[4] "America's Most Decorated Woman Fought from the Philippines to Korea," We Are The Mighty.
[5] "Women in the Air Force—Displays in Korean War Gallery," National Museum of the U.S. Air Force.
[6] "Obituary: Janice Feagin Britton, BSN '44, Nurse on Three Continents," Vanderbilt University; "Janice Warrene Feagin Olson Britton," NDH Silent Heroes.
[7] Eileen A. Bjorkman, review of Fly Girls Revolt: The Story of the Women Who Kicked Open the Door to Fly in Combat, National Defense University Foundation, July 16, 2023.
[8] "The History of the Navy Nurse Corps," Naval History and Heritage Command; "Lashed Together, 10 Nurses Survive; They Credit Medical Officer Who Tied Them to Plank," New York Times, August 27, 1950.

Chapter 7— Vietnam: Conflict at Home and Overseas

"In the rice paddies of Vietnam, the whispers of history echo through the winds."

– Duong Thu Huong

THE VIETNAM WAR GREW out of an older struggle over empire and a newer struggle over the Cold War.

After World War II, Vietnamese nationalists fought to end French colonial rule, winning a 1954 partition that split the country along the 17th parallel: a communist North and a U.S.-backed South. Instead of allowing nationwide elections that might reunify Vietnam, American leaders, fearing the spread of communism in Asia, chose to support South Vietnam with money, weapons, and advisers, turning a decolonization conflict into a frontline of U.S. containment policy.

What began as "advising" and support missions slowly escalated. In 1964, after disputed incidents in the Gulf of Tonkin, Congress gave President Lyndon Johnson broad authority to use force, and U.S. involvement widened from backing South Vietnamese troops to flying bombing campaigns and sending ground combat units.

By the late 1960s, hundreds of thousands of American troops were deployed in a war that stretched from rice paddies and jungle firebases to cities like Saigon and Hue. It was a conflict without a formal declaration of war, fought within limits that sought to confine it to Southeast Asia while still demanding continuous combat operations.

This war blurred boundaries that had shaped earlier conflicts. There was no clear front line; guerrilla tactics, ambushes, and search-and-destroy missions mixed with large-scale conventional battles. Intelligence estimates, target lists, aerial photography, and the constant movement of people and materiel through an immense administrative and operational apparatus shaped decisions. The battlefield was dispersed, mobile, and often invisible, and so was much of the labor that sustained it.

Airpower and helicopters made mobility a core part of strategy, while television and photography brought images of fighting and casualties into American homes in near real time. The United States relied on a massive support structure that stretched from field hospitals in Vietnam to bases in the Pacific and across the continental United States. Within that machinery, women played a larger and more varied role than in any previous American war, even though the law still barred them from most combat assignments.

Vietnam was both a battlefield and a political storm. It was a war that became deeply unpopular at home, sparked intense protest, and ended without a clear victory. Yet, it also pushed the armed forces toward new levels of technical complexity and professionalization.

Women's service was woven into that system. In Vietnam, women's roles ranged from front-line medical care and air evacuation to behind-the-scenes intelligence and communications, and from officially uniformed service to civilian and local participation—making them part of nearly every layer of the war's machinery, even as the law kept them formally out of combat arms.

They served as air traffic controllers, radio and teletype operators, weather and radar specialists, and administrative staff in headquarters and operations centers in Vietnam and nearby countries, including Thailand, Japan, Guam, and the Philippines, roles that directly shaped flight safety, targeting, and command decisions. Thousands more women served through organizations such as the American Red Cross, USO, and Army Special Services, providing recreation, counseling, and a psychological link to home.

Vietnam reshaped what it meant for women to serve in an unpopular, televised, and deeply contested war.

Doris Ilda Allen - The Woman Who Warned the Army About the Tet Offensive

Doris Ilda "Lucki" Allen was born in 1927 in Mobile, Alabama. She joined the Women's Army Corps in the late 1940s, at a time when both her race and her gender marked her as an exception within the institution she was entering. She stayed anyway, threading her way into the small, demanding world of Army intelligence.

She completed French-language training and then broke a barrier: she became the first woman to attend the Prisoner of War Interrogation course at the U.S. Army Intelligence School, qualifying not as a clerk or support worker, but as someone trained to extract information from captured enemy personnel under pressure.

Doris Allen, Public Domain

In 1967, Doris went to Vietnam. Her initial assignment drew directly on that training: she deployed as a POW interrogator, working in the overlapping domains of questioning prisoners, exploiting captured documents, and feeding what she learned into the Army's intelligence system. This meant long hours with detainees and stacks of paper—interviews about unit structures, routes, caches, and plans; notebooks and maps taken from dead or captured enemy soldiers; and reports that had to be sifted and translated into usable leads.

As an African American WAC in a male-dominated field, she was already an outlier. As someone whose job was to listen closely to the enemy and then decide what mattered, she was also at the heart of how the war was being fought.

Over time, she shifted into a broader analytical role. As a Senior Intelligence Analyst at the Army Operations Center in Long Binh, a major U.S. headquarters complex outside Saigon, she moved from handling one case at a time to tracking patterns: spikes in enemy activity along specific routes, changes in the tone and content of intercepted communications, and movements of units that deviated from the usual rhythms. Her job was to turn scattered reports, including interrogation summaries, patrol debriefs, and captured documents, into assessments that commanders could use to plan operations or prepare for attacks.

One episode illustrates the stakes of that work. According to contemporary reporting, Doris's analysis in late 1967 pointed to a significant, coordinated enemy offensive: she identified indicators that North Vietnamese and Viet Cong forces were preparing something larger than routine attacks, and she warned of the possibility of widespread strikes during the coming holiday period. Her written warning correctly anticipated elements of what became the Tet Offensive in early 1968—but the account notes that her report was discounted and not acted on at higher levels.[1]

When Tet finally erupted, with simultaneous attacks across South Vietnam that shocked the American public and leadership, it underscored both how sharp her analysis had been and how fragile the link between intelligence and decision-making could be.

Doris was not an abstraction; she was a Black woman in a WAC uniform performing the core work of the war: interrogation, document exploitation, pattern recognition, and warning. Her career shows that women, including women of color, were already in the rooms where information was turned into assessments, even if their names rarely appeared in official narratives. It also illustrates a central tension in Vietnam: having good intelligence did not guarantee that leaders would listen.

For her service in Vietnam, Doris was awarded three Bronze Stars. After returning to the U.S., she became the first full-time female instructor in prisoner interrogation at the Army Intelligence Center and later served as a counterintelligence specialist. After her retirement in 1980, she was inducted into the Military Intelligence Hall of Fame, becoming just the second Black woman to receive that recognition.

But her legacy is bittersweet: Doris did what the system asked of her—learn languages, master interrogation, analyze the data, and write the warning—and yet watched helplessly as an offensive she had foreseen crashed into a country that believed it was winning.

Brig. Gen. Wilma L. Vaught (USAF) – Women in Command

Wilma L. Vaught went to Vietnam not with a rifle platoon, but with a calculator and a clearance badge—and that was precisely what made her dangerous to the old rules.

Born in 1930 and commissioned into the Air Force in 1957, she built her early career in the comptroller field, specializing in management analysis: the unglamorous, numbers-heavy work of determining whether plans, budgets, and operations aligned. By the time she finished graduate school at the University of Alabama in 1968, the Air Force sent her where that skill mattered most: Saigon, to the sprawling headquarters of the Military Assistance Command, Vietnam (MACV).

MACV was the brain and nervous system of the American war effort in Vietnam—an enormous, layered headquarters that turned Washington's strategy into daily orders, budgets, and metrics. Wilma spent a year there as a management analyst. In practice, that meant reading everything. In her oral history, she describes arriving at MACV and simply working through every file in the comptroller's office until she was the only person who really knew what was in them.[2]

Every battalion rotation, every base expansion, and every new logistics hub or advisory detachment had to be funded, justified, and tracked. As a management analyst and comptroller staff officer, she sat at the intersection of resources and reality. If a unit was burning through supplies faster than expected, a program was underperforming, or audit findings pointed to waste or mismanagement, it was her job to surface it, translate it into numbers and charts, and push it up the chain.

In a war increasingly judged by body counts, sortie rates, and dollars spent, she worked within the machinery that produced those numbers—and that, in turn, shaped how Washington and Saigon believed the war was going.

Even getting to Vietnam required her to work around gender restrictions. No one prepared her for a combat zone. She recalls that before Saigon, "they taught me absolutely nothing" about going to war. Women in her specialty were rarely given weapons training, even though MACV was a war-zone headquarters that came under rocket and mortar fire. So she went home on leave, found her brother-in-law—"very skilled with weapons"—and asked him to teach her to shoot.

On an improvised range, she practiced with a rifle and a handgun, firing prone and standing, until he told her she had effectively qualified as an expert. A sympathetic woman at the range later quietly left her ammunition and weapons, telling her she "might need" them in Vietnam. She carried those privately obtained weapons through her tour, a quiet act of self-protection in a system that would pay her combat pay but had not thought it necessary to teach her to defend herself.

Her postwar career was also impressive. She was the first woman to deploy with an Air Force bomber unit and the first to reach the rank of brigadier general from the comptroller field. She became concerned that the role of women in the military was going unnoticed, and pushed for a memorial as the leader of the Women in Military Service to America Memorial Foundation. This resulted in the Women in Military Service for America Memorial being built at the entrance to Arlington National Cemetery.

In 2000, Wilma was inducted into the National Women's Hall of Fame.

Controlling the Skies

Vietnam was not only fought in jungles and rice paddies; it was sustained by an aviation system whose safety, tempo, and throughput depended on controllers—often young, often overruled socially, but operationally non-negotiable.

Sandra Durbin

Sandra Durbin signed her Navy enlistment papers in 1966, a teenager's mix of nerves and determination, trading three years of service for the promise of four years of college tuition. The deal seemed straightforward: serve, study, and step into a better future. But the path she chose—air traffic control—would put her under a harsher spotlight than she could have imagined, where every mistake could cost lives and every success would be questioned because of who she was, not what she could do.

After boot camp, her test scores opened doors that had long been closed to women, especially Black women. She qualified for one of the Navy's most demanding technical tracks: air traffic control. The pressure would be immense: she was entering a field where a single wrong call from the tower could turn an ordinary flight line into wreckage and fire.

Her first taste of that pressure came before she ever reached an operational tower. With racial tensions at their peak, women faced tremendous prejudice for joining the military in the 1960s.

When she reported to the air traffic control school in December 1966, she was pulled into a Captain's Mast the very day she arrived, a disciplinary proceeding usually reserved for sailors who had already broken the rules. She had not. Her "offense" was walking through the door as a Black woman assigned to a job that many around her believed should belong only to men—white men at that.

In that room, rank and authority were stacked against her. She was accused of cheating on her tests, as though the Navy could not imagine her earning her scores honestly, and she was told she might be pulled from training and shunted into what they called "women's work". The message beneath the words was clear: this job is not for you; this responsibility is too much for someone like you.[3]

Without power or allies to push back directly, Sandra reached for the only tool she controlled: performance. She studied when she was supposed to and when she was not, attending mandatory remedial study sessions even though she had not been assigned to them. When she graduated, she ranked among the top of her class, converting doubt and skepticism into something harder to dismiss—a quiet, undeniable record of achievement.

That momentum carried beyond the classroom. She moved swiftly through the enlisted ranks, earning the rank of petty officer (E-4) while still a teenager. With each new stripe came greater authority and steeper consequences. In the control tower, her voice carried the weight of aircraft, fuel, and human lives, guiding them safely through open air and narrow margins of error.

Once she reached operational air traffic control, her work stopped being symbolic and became brutally real. The tower is a narrow bridge between order and disaster, a place where routine can flip into emergency with a single radio call, and Sandra stood on that bridge, headset on, responsible for keeping aircraft and vehicles separated by seconds and feet instead of miles. Every instruction—hold short, cleared for takeoff, cross the runway—carried the weight of knowing that if she hesitated, bent, or guessed, someone might not go home.

Being a "first" also carried a daily reckoning that rarely made headlines. Even though she was not in the cockpit, she occupied a seat where a single mistake could take down a pilot, a crew, and everyone on board. The tension of that responsibility sat atop another burden: knowing that if anything went wrong, some people would blame not the chaos of aviation, fog, or malfunction, but her race and gender.

Sandra is recognized as the first Black female air traffic controller in the U.S. Navy, and in some accounts, as the first Black female air traffic controller in the United States. After Sandra completed Navy ATC training, Eleanor Williams later became the FAA's first Black female air traffic controller. This detail underscores how Durbin's breakthrough in uniform came before the better-known civilian milestone.

The story beneath the title "first" is not tidy. It is the story of a young woman who walked into a system that expected her to fail, and who carried the double weight of technical responsibility and social doubt every time she keyed her microphone. Her legacy lives not only in plaques and articles, but in every moment when a controller, regardless of race or gender, gives a hard "no" on a busy frequency and holds the line because safety—not ego, not pressure—must win.

Sandra Durbin

The Workhorse of Vietnam: Sky Nurses

The Vietnam War turned the sky itself into a hospital corridor. Helicopters and fixed-wing aircraft became the arteries of a new medical system that pulled casualties from jungle clearings and city streets, rushed them through surgical teams, and then carried them onward to larger hospitals in Vietnam, the Pacific, and the United States.

Within that chain, Air Force nurses served as flight nurses on two main types of missions: short "intratheater" hops moving the wounded between facilities within the combat zone and longer flights ferrying patients out of Vietnam altogether.

By the mid-1960s, women in the Air Force Nurse Corps were flying these missions routinely, turning transport aircraft into moving wards where the senior medical authority was often a nurse with a clipboard, a stethoscope, and a cabin full of patients at altitude.

Flight nurses managed entire cabins of patients in thin air, heat and cold, and deafening noise, with equipment that had to be lashed down and checked constantly. On a typical mission, a flight nurse and a small team of aeromedical technicians monitored shock, bleeding, pain, burns, respiratory distress, and fragile post-operative vital signs, adjusting oxygen, IV fluids, and medications while keeping detailed records for the next receiving team.

If a patient crashed in flight, there was no backup department to call; the nurse led the response, improvising with what fit in a medical kit and what the aircraft's power and space would allow.

Bernadette "Bernie" Sanner

Bernadette "Bernie" Sanner grew up in East Chicago, Indiana, with a specific dream in mind. From childhood, she wanted to be a nurse, a path her Polish immigrant grandmother, Sophie, quietly helped set in motion. Bernie remembered talking with Sophie about nursing and only later learned that her grandmother had set up an annuity in her name. By the time she finished high school, the money for nursing school was already waiting, a gift Sophie never boasted about but had carefully planned.

After graduation, Bernie entered a three-year nursing program in Hammond, Indiana. By her third year of training, the wider world was pulling at her. Every branch of the military seemed to be courting student nurses, taking them on day trips, offering to pay for further schooling in exchange for enlistment, and making it clear how badly they needed trained nurses for Vietnam.

At 22, she joined the Air Force. Her officer training was short—only a couple of weeks in San Antonio learning the basics of military customs and leadership—before she moved to Dyess Air Force Base in Abilene, Texas, for her first year of service. Texas was her introduction to Air Force culture, but Vietnam arrived quickly.

On July 1, 1968, Bernie left Seattle, Washington, on a flight that would take three days and land her at Cam Ranh Bay. The Air Force had begun assigning women nurses to Vietnam in 1966. By the time she arrived, female flight nurses were already flying aeromedical evacuation missions, turning aircraft into mobile wards for wounded service members. At Cam Ranh, Bernie joined a vast base that hosted units from every branch—Army, Navy, Air Force, Marines. The hospital sat near the flight line so nurses and medics could move patients directly onto transport planes, preparing them for evacuation to larger facilities in Japan, the Philippines, or back to the United States.

Bernadette Sanner

Day-to-day, her work was relentless. In her unit, doctors were physically present only a few days a week; most of the time, they were in the operating rooms. They issued orders and treatment plans, and the nurses carried them out primarily on their own.

Bernie and her colleagues stabilized wounded soldiers, managed pain, dressed wounds, monitored for shock and infection, and prepared patients to be loaded onto aircraft. Mortar attacks hit the base every few months. Still, the hospital kept operating, its proximity to the runway a reminder that the war's front lines now ran straight through the evacuation system.

The schedule was as punishing as the work. Nurses at Cam Ranh Bay worked 12-hour shifts for seven days straight—7 a.m. to 7 p.m.—then had a single day off to flip to nights, followed by another seven days of 7 p.m. to 7 a.m. duty. That rhythm blurred days and nights into a continuous stream of patients and flights.

These women functioned as the steady center of a system that could not afford to stop, even when the sky over the base brightened with incoming fire.

The Ultimate Cost of Service

More than 265,000 American women served in the U.S. military during the Vietnam era, and about 10,000–11,000 of them served in Vietnam or Southeast Asia itself. Close to 90 percent of those in-country military service women worked in medical roles, primarily as nurses, facing mass-casualty days that blurred into nights. Members of the Army Nurse Corps were in Vietnam as early as 1956 to train Vietnamese women in nursing skills. By 1963, larger numbers of Army Corps Nurses arrived in Vietnam. Over the years, these women worked long hours to aid the servicemembers killed and injured in war.

Guerilla warfare made it impossible to be safe behind the lines, as women received injuries during battle, both visible and invisible. Air Force nurses participated in air evacuation missions. Navy women served on hospital ships such as USS Repose and USS Sanctuary off the coast of Vietnam.

The Women on the Wall

Eight American military women died in the Vietnam War, and every one of them was a nurse whose name is etched on the Vietnam Veterans Memorial. Most of these women were lost in aircraft or helicopter crashes—classic Vietnam hazards that struck even far from the front lines.

Civilian Women in Harm's Way

The loss does not stop with uniforms. American women serving as civilians—especially in aid, medical, and support roles with organizations and U.S. agencies—also died because of the war. Official counts vary slightly, but multiple sources converge on about 65 American civilian women killed in connection with the Vietnam War.[4]

First Lt. Sharon Ann Lane

First Lt. Sharon Ann Lane was a young Army nurse whose courage and love for her patients cost her life during a rocket attack on her hospital in Vietnam in 1969. She became the only American servicewoman in the Vietnam War killed directly by enemy fire and was honored after her death for her heroism.

Sharon was born on July 7, 1943, in Canton, Ohio, where she grew up in a close-knit family and dreamed of becoming a nurse. After high school, she trained at the Aultman Hospital School of Nursing, earning a reputation for being steady, kind, and dependable with patients.

Even before joining the Army, she was drawn to service, working long hours in civilian hospitals and showing a calm under pressure that others noticed. Friends and colleagues remembered her as soft-spoken yet strong-willed, someone who quietly did the hard work without seeking attention.

On April 18, 1968, Sharon joined the U.S. Army Nurse Corps Reserve and soon began medical training at Brooke Army Medical Center in Texas. She completed the course in June, was commissioned as a second lieutenant, and then reported to Fitzsimons General Hospital in Denver.

After being promoted to first lieutenant, she handled demanding assignments at Fitzsimons, first on tuberculosis wards and then in the cardiac intensive care unit and recovery room. When the chance came to volunteer for overseas duty, she asked to go, accepting orders to Vietnam in the spring of 1969.

Sharon arrived in South Vietnam on April 24, 1969, and reported to the Army's 312th Evacuation Hospital in Chu Lai a few days later. Her first assignment was in the intensive care unit, but she soon transferred to the Vietnamese ward, where she cared for local civilians, soldiers, and prisoners of war.[5]

The work took a steady toll, both physical and emotional. When opportunities arose to transfer to safer, less demanding assignments, she declined them, choosing instead to remain with her patients. Her days settled into a brutal rhythm: twelve-hour shifts in the Vietnamese ward, five days a week, followed by what passed for free time—

hours spent helping the most critically wounded American soldiers in the surgical ICU.

Just after dawn on June 8, 1969, that routine was shattered. A barrage of 122-millimeter rockets slammed into the 312th Evacuation Hospital at Chu Lai, bringing the war crashing directly into the place meant to hold it at bay.

Sharon Ann Lane

One rocket exploded between two Quonset huts that formed the Vietnamese ward where Lane worked, killing two people and wounding twenty-seven others.

When the first rockets began to fall, Sharon did not run for shelter; she rushed toward her ward, thinking only of protecting her patients from the incoming fire. A rocket blast sent metal fragments into her chest, killing her instantly, just one month before her twenty-sixth birthday.

Legacy and Honors

For her actions that day, Lane was posthumously awarded the Bronze Star Medal with a "V" device for valor, recognizing her heroism in rushing to her patients under attack. She also received the Purple Heart, the National Defense Service Medal, the Vietnam Service Medal, the National Order of Vietnam, and the Vietnamese Gallantry Cross with Palm.

While eight American military nurses died while serving in Vietnam, Sharon Ann Lane was the only American servicewoman killed directly by hostile fire, a fact that made her story stand out nationwide. Memorials in her honor stand in Ohio, and her name is etched on Panel 23W, Line 112 of the Vietnam Veterans Memorial Wall in Washington, D.C., where visitors come to remember the young nurse who chose to run toward danger for her patients.

Captain Mary Therese Klinker – Operation Babylift

Captain Mary Therese Klinker brought women's service into the war's final, chaotic act. A member of the U.S. Air

Force Nurse Corps, she served as a flight nurse in the later years of the conflict. In April 1975, she was assigned to one of the war's most symbolically charged missions: Operation Babylift, a rapid evacuation of Vietnamese orphans and other children as Saigon neared collapse.

On April 4, 1975, Mary boarded the first Babylift flight from Tan Son Nhut Air Base, helping load, secure, and care for children and caregivers aboard a crowded C-5A Galaxy that combined medical evacuation with emergency humanitarian transport. Shortly after takeoff, a catastrophic structural failure forced the aircraft into a crash landing; Mary was killed while attempting to bring the plane and its passengers down.[6]

Her death laid bare realities that official categories tried to soften. She is widely recognized as the only member of the U.S. Air Force Nurse Corps killed in the Vietnam War and the last American nurse to die during that conflict's operational period, a fact that undermines any easy distinction between "combat" and "support" when support occurs in contested airspace.

In the aftermath, she was posthumously awarded the Airman's Medal for heroism, a rare and explicit acknowledgment that flight nursing required the same courage under fire as the more visible combat decorations celebrated.

Her story weaves together the era's themes: a medical system built on constant motion, women placed at the center of life-and-death decision-making within that system, and an institution that only fully recognized the danger and value of their work in the language of medals and memorials after they were gone.

Vietnam's flight nurses made the evacuation chain function, and their work turned aircraft into medical systems—fast, fragile, and lifesaving—inside a war that rarely stayed contained to the ground.

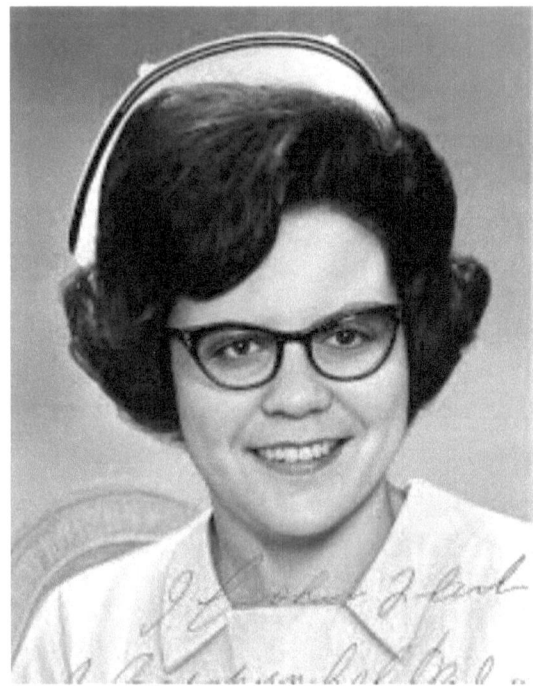

Mary Therese Klinker

---

[1] William Beterbide, "Army Veteran Doris Allen," March 22, 2024.
[2] "Brigadier General Wilma L. Vaught," United States Air Force.
[3] "Sandra Durbin," National Air Traffic Controllers Association.
[4] "Women in Vietnam," Vietnam Veterans Memorial Fund.
[5] "The American Military Women Who Lost Their Lives in Vietnam," Time, May 27, 2021.
[6] "Two AF Nurses: Heroes of Operation Babylift," U.S. Air Force.

Chapter 8 — Between Wars: Women and the Cold War's Turning Point

"To strive, to seek, to find, and not to yield."

— Alfred, Lord Tennyson

The Post-Vietnam Reset and the Cold War World Women Entered

THE VIETNAM WAR ENDED without triumph, without clarity, and without consensus. For the U.S. military, the withdrawal in 1973 marked not simply the end of a conflict but the collapse of an entire operating model.

The draft—long the backbone of American manpower—was politically and socially exhausted. Public trust in military leadership had eroded. The armed forces faced shrinking ranks, morale problems, and a legitimacy crisis at home.

Out of that rupture came a structural reset. In 1973, the United States transitioned to an All-Volunteer Force, betting that professionalism, incentives, and long-term careers could replace conscription. This was not an abstract reform. It forced the services to rethink who could serve, how long they would stay, and which barriers were no longer sustainable.

Women—historically treated as temporary auxiliaries or wartime exceptions—became part of the manpower solution rather than a symbolic presence.

At the same time, the world had not grown safer. The Cold War defined the post-Vietnam era not through declared battles but through enduring tension. The United States and the Soviet Union did not fight each other directly; instead, they confronted one another through nuclear standoffs, proxy conflicts, intelligence operations, and global military readiness.

Europe remained divided by ideology and arms. Korea remained frozen in armistice, not peace. New crises flared in the Middle East, Africa, and Central America. War was no longer episodic—it was continuous, anticipatory, and bureaucratic.

This was a military built less for jungle combat than for deterrence: maintaining readiness, guarding alliances, projecting stability, and preparing for a war everyone hoped would never come but trained for relentlessly. Bases, commands, logistics networks, intelligence systems, and air power became central. So did careers measured in decades rather than deployments measured in months.

For women in uniform, this environment created both opportunity and constraint. The Cold War military needed skilled personnel who could be trained, retained, and trusted over time. That reality pushed the services to open doors—to academies, to technical specialties, to permanent commissions. Yet those openings came with limits. Women were integrated, but cautiously. They were relied upon, but regulated. Policies governing marriage, pregnancy, and parenthood reflected an institution still unsure whether women were full participants or provisional ones.

The Cold War years were not as dramatic as Korea or Vietnam had been. There were no mass demobilizations, no iconic surrender scenes. Instead, change came quietly: through legislation, executive orders, recruiting manuals, training pipelines, and personnel rules. By the late 1980s, the result was a force that looked very different from the one that left Saigon—more professional, more diverse, and structurally prepared for women to serve at scale.

That preparation would be tested not in theory, but in 1991, when the United States went to war again—this time with women fully embedded across the force.

The Cracks Begin

By 1976, the walls keeping women out of long-term military careers were cracking. Court rulings and new laws were breaking down barriers that had kept women from full integration into the military.

One new law was aimed at leadership. In October 1975, President Gerald Ford signed Public Law 94-106, which opened the doors of America's service academies—West Point, the Naval Academy, the Air Force Academy, and others—to women for the first time in history.[1]

The change became real the following summer. On a warm July morning in 1976, 119 young women gathered at the gates of West Point alongside more than a thousand men. They carried the same heavy duffel bags, wore the same stiff new uniforms, and braced themselves for the same shouted orders that had shaped generations of cadets before them. But unlike anyone who came before, these young women were walking into something entirely new. There was no roadmap for them—no older female graduates to look up to, no guarantees their peers or instructors would even accept them.

Every step they took up those stone steps was a quiet act of courage. Some faced open skepticism; others endured isolation. Yet together, they began something that would ripple through the decades. These pioneering women weren't just earning an education—they were claiming the right to lead, command, and shape the military's future from the inside.

1980 West Point Graduating Class

They also weren't there to make a statement. They were there to belong. And over the next four years, they did far more than that. They competed, led, and proved that excellence had no gender.

Andrea Hollen, Class of 1980

At their 1980 graduation, one cadet in particular came to symbolize what that first class had achieved. Andrea Hollen became the first woman to cross the stage and receive her diploma. She wasn't just first alphabetically—she was, by all accounts, among the top-ranked Marines in the class. For West Point, her moment on that stage marked a visible break from nearly two centuries of tradition.[2]

Andrea Hollen

Hollen's accomplishments went even further. She was the class's only Rhodes Scholar that year—a singular, unmistakable mark of intellectual achievement. Her success forced the academy, and by extension the nation, to confront a powerful truth: the first women weren't tokens filling a new quota. They were competitors, leaders, and scholars who thrived under the same pressure that had defined generations of cadets before them.

The experience of Hollen and her classmates reshaped the institution from within. West Point, long a symbol of rigid military tradition, had to reconcile its heritage with undeniable performance. Slowly, the idea of women as "exceptions" faded, replaced by something more enduring: respect earned through results.

This moment marked a profound cultural shift. The academies weren't just schools—they were the main pipelines to the military's upper ranks. When the doors opened to women, it set in motion a slow but powerful transformation that took root in the 1980s and 1990s. Many of the high-ranking women who later broke barriers—colonels, generals, admirals—traced their paths back to this first generation of students who refused to accept that leadership was a man's domain.

Cushman v Crawford, 1976

But there was still an obstacle standing in many women's way of fully embracing a life of service: if you became pregnant, your career was over.

This wasn't just an unspoken custom—it was the law. A 1951 executive order granted the armed services full authority to discharge any woman who became pregnant or gave birth. The result was predictably devastating. Women who wanted to serve their country were routinely forced out, stripped of their income, benefits, and careers.

It didn't matter if they wanted to keep serving. Pregnancy was proof that you didn't belong. For many women, it felt like the institution they had sworn to serve had turned its back the moment their private lives became visible.

Everything began to change in 1976 because one woman decided to fight back. Her name was Mary Crawford, a Marine who was discharged simply because she became pregnant. She took her case—Crawford v. Cushman—all the way to the U.S. Court of Appeals.

On February 23, 1976, the court handed down a groundbreaking decision: the Marine Corps' policy of mandatory pregnancy discharge was unconstitutional. It violated the fundamental rights of women who had volunteered to serve.

That ruling became another opening, and through it came the beginning of something new. The Cushman decision, along with the earlier acceptance of women at academies, forced the military to rethink its treatment of female servicemembers. Women could remain in uniform, advance in rank, attend military schools, and build long-term careers, even while raising children.

This shift didn't instantly make the military a welcoming place for mothers. But it did something subtler and more profound: it marked the beginning of recognizing women not as temporary helpers but as true career soldiers, sailors, and Marines.

In the story of women's military service, 1976 was a pivotal year: women finally had a fighting chance to stay, serve, and rise—on their own terms. Together, those two changes—the right to remain in uniform while also being a mother, and the right to enter the academies—rewrote what a woman's military life could look like.

The End of WAC

But more change was coming. By the mid-1970s, the military was in the midst of a quiet revolution. The old barriers—laws, traditions, and unspoken rules—were falling one by one. The final symbol of the "separate tracks" era disappeared on October 20, 1978, when the Women's Army Corps (WAC) was officially disbanded.

For more than three decades, the WAC had been the only way women could serve in the Army. It gave them uniforms, ranks, and pride—but also kept them apart. WAC members worked in their own offices, trained in their own units, and even had a separate chain of command. The message was clear: women could assist the Army, but they weren't the Army.

When the WAC was absorbed into the regular Army in 1978, it was more than an administrative change. It was the military's way of finally saying that women were soldiers too—part of the same force, governed by the same rules, and held to the same standards. But it was also complicated. The integration didn't erase prejudice or open every door. Women were still barred from combat roles and often faced bias from peers who didn't yet want them "in the line."

Even so, this was a turning point. The end of the WAC ushered in the era of structural inclusion. By the 1980s, women were no longer standing outside the system—they were working within it, shaping its future.

Let Them Fly

In the late 1970s and 1980s, the Air Force sky slowly started to change. For decades, women who could fly had been kept at the margins—good enough to train, ferry, or teach, but not fully welcomed as pilots in the regular force. That began to shift in 1976, when women were admitted to the Air Force Academy and accepted into the Air Force on roughly the same basis as men.

Opening the Door to the Cockpit

Legal and policy changes laid the groundwork before any woman ever strapped into a test jet.

In 1967, Public Law 90-130 removed caps on the number of women who could serve and lifted some promotion limits, making it possible for more women to build real careers. In the mid-1970s, the Air Force launched a test program to train women as pilots; the first 10 female Air Force pilots earned their silver wings on September 2, 1977, flying alongside male classmates.

Women were still barred from combat missions by law, but now they could wear wings, fly military aircraft, and move into roles that had once been completely closed to them.

From "Let them Fly" to "Prove they Belong"

Once that door cracked open, a new kind of woman officer stepped through—highly trained, technically sharp, and willing to live under a microscope in the cockpit.

By the late 1980s and early 1990s, women officers were moving into demanding flight test roles, including at the U.S. Air Force Test Pilot School at Edwards Air Force Base.

Susan Jane Helms

Officers like Susan Helms, who graduated from the Air Force Academy in 1980 and became a distinguished graduate of the Test Pilot School as a flight test engineer, showed how women could excel in some of the Air Force's most technical and elite flying environments.

These women were not just "allowed" to fly; they were asked to help push aircraft and systems to their limits—exactly the kind of work that proved whether an airframe, or a person, could handle the pressure.

Her world was one of checklists, data points, and split-second decisions—flying test profiles that demanded absolute precision while knowing any mistake could be used as "proof" women didn't belong in the cockpit.

From New Cadet to Weapons Engineer

After commissioning, she went to Eglin Air Force Base in Florida as an F-16 weapons separation engineer with the Air Force Armament Laboratory, testing how bombs and missiles left the aircraft in flight.

By 1982, she was the lead engineer for F-15 weapons separation—an early sign that a woman officer could be trusted with critical, highly technical work on front-line fighter systems.

From the start, her arena was the intersection of engineering, flight, and lethality—the core of how the Air Force fought in the 1980s.

Scholar and Teacher in Uniform

The Air Force then invested in her mind as much as her test work. Selected for graduate school, she earned an advanced degree in aeronautics and astronautics from Stanford University in 1985.

After graduating, she returned to the Academy as an assistant professor of aeronautics, teaching the next wave of cadets—men and women—how aircraft and space systems actually work.

She was both a product of integration and a builder of it, shaping the education of future officers in the very institution that had only recently opened to women.

Flight Test Engineer and the Cold Lake Years

In 1987, Susan took another step into elite territory when she was selected for the U.S. Air Force Test Pilot School at Edwards Air Force Base. After a year of intensive training as a Flight Test Engineer, she became a U.S. Air Force exchange officer at the Aerospace Engineering Test Establishment. There, she worked on the CF-18 program as a Flight Test Engineer and project officer, managing the development of a simulation of the CF-18 flight control system for the Canadian Forces.[3]

Over the course of this work, she flew in 30 different types of U.S. and Canadian military aircraft—an unmistakable record of trust placed in her technical judgment and performance.

From Test Ranges to Space

Susan's test work and engineering expertise led directly to her selection as a NASA astronaut. She turned the Cold War military's hunger for engineers and test professionals into a literal launchpad beyond Earth.

Susan Helms

She was promoted to brigadier general in 2006 and was given command of the 45th Space Wing at Patrick Air Force Base, which is responsible for launching U.S. government and commercial satellites from Cape Canaveral.

She later rose to the rank of Commander, Joint Functional Component Command for Space, leading more than 20,000 personnel on missions such as missile warning, space situational awareness, satellite operations, and space launch and range operations.

In other words, she went from one of the first women to walk the terrazzo at the Academy to the three-star general responsible for the United States' day-to-day space operations—a straight, documented line from integration in the late 1970s to women holding institutional power in the information and space age.

But she did more than advance her own career; she quietly rewrote expectations about what women could do in high-stakes aviation, flight testing not only airplanes but also the institution's willingness to judge her by performance rather than by stereotype.

Women were now part of keeping the Air Force's weapons and systems safer and more effective, and proving over and over that skill, not gender, was what kept a plane in the air.

Rear Admiral Grace Murray Hopper

The military entering the Reagan years was no longer defined solely by tanks, missiles, and manpower. It was now powered by information: computers, code, and the systems that linked global command networks. One of the people who led that transformation was Rear Admiral Grace Murray Hopper.

Grace's Navy career reads like a map of technological progress. A mathematician and computer pioneer, she was part of the earliest efforts to program the machines that would become modern computers. Long before "digital transformation" became a buzzword, she was living it—writing code, standardizing languages, and pushing a data-driven Navy into the information age.

Her promotions tell their own story: she became a captain in 1973, a commodore in 1983, and a rear admiral in 1985—a leap few women of her generation ever made, and one that came at a moment when the term "cyberspace" was still science fiction.[4] That 1983 promotion, approved during the Reagan administration, reflected more than a personal milestone. It symbolized the military's growing recognition that the future of national defense depended not only on force but also on information and strategy.

The late 1970s had broken barriers to entry, and the 1980s, and women like Grace showed what women could build once they were inside.

Andrea Motley

In 1982, a young sergeant named Andrea Motley stepped onto a dive deck knowing she did not look like anyone else there—she was the only woman, the only Black soldier, and the only person in that space who, in the eyes of many around her, was never meant to belong.[5] The Army's deep-sea diving community was small, elite, and almost entirely white and male.

In her 1982 class at the U.S. Navy Deep Sea Diving and Salvage Training Center in Florida, Andrea was the only woman and the only Black student among dozens of men.

The course was brutal—physically punishing, technically demanding—and designed to wash out anyone who couldn't keep up.

Andrea did more than keep up. She became the first female deep-sea diver in the U.S. Army and the first Black female deep-sea diver in any branch of the U.S. military. Her badge was not merely a qualification; it was proof that the limits others saw were not the limits of her ability.

Earning the title did not mean earning acceptance.

At her first assignment, some fellow divers made it clear she wasn't welcome—turning off her air underwater as a "joke," leaving a dead snake in the freezer, walking around naked after workouts, and assigning her deliberately impossible tasks. Andrea's daily reality was a mix of danger and disrespect: she faced the usual risks of deep-sea work and the added risk that someone on her own team might try to rattle or undermine her.

She had to prove herself "over and over and over again every day," not just as a diver, but as a Black woman in a space that had never imagined someone like her in its ranks.

The Cost of Being First

Even as she excelled, Andrea ran into a wall she could not break.

Orders for advanced training disappeared, her perfect fitness scores were rescored against male standards to undercut her, and then came the blow: the Army closed her diving specialty to women again. When she filed discrimination complaints, every office she turned to told her there was nothing they could do.

Finally, she asked to be relieved of dive duty. She left angry, not because she had failed, but because she had succeeded and was still pushed out of the work she loved.

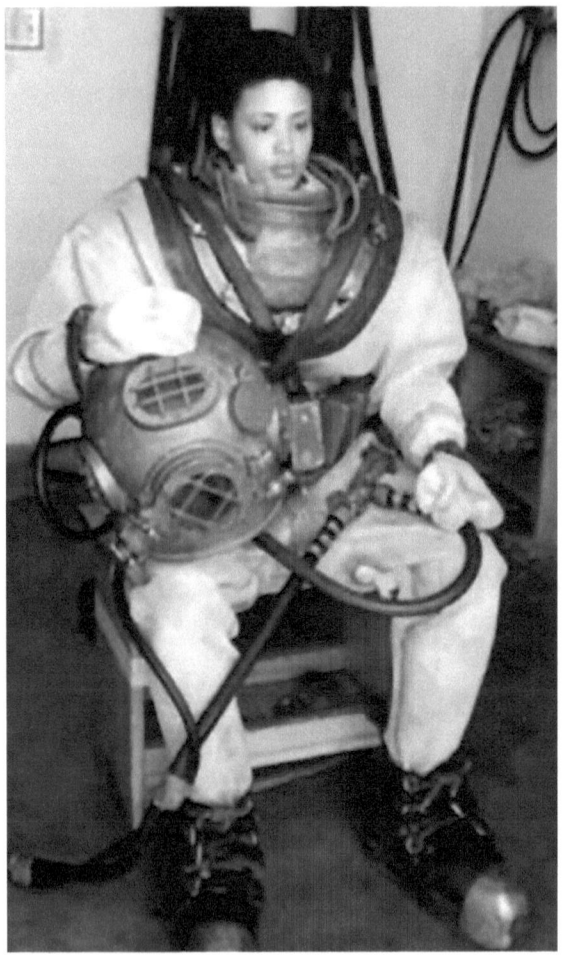

Andrea Motley

Andrea Motley's story shows what the 1980s really looked like for many women in uniform: doors opening just wide enough to slip through, only to slam shut again when they did too well.

On paper, she was precisely what the post–1970s reforms were supposed to make possible—a Black woman in a highly skilled, high-risk specialty. In practice, her experience exposed how fragile those gains were while prejudice and institutional fear remained.

Heading into the 1990s

By the end of the 1980s, the transformation that began in the mid-1970s had fully taken root. The military that entered the next decade looked fundamentally different from the one that had expelled women for pregnancy, closed the academies' gates, and confined them to auxiliary corps.

Women were no longer the exception. They were engineers pushing fighter designs to their limits, divers braving the cold seas, test pilots climbing into supersonic jets, and scientists building the information and space systems that defined military power in the modern age. These decades had been about constructing the scaffolding—laws, roles, and credibility—that would eventually test women when conflict came.

Until this moment, women had served bravely, yet always one step removed from the front lines. The Cold War was long, intense, and global—but mostly cold. No one yet knew what these changes would mean when the battlefield went hot again.

That answer came in 1990 when Iraq invaded Kuwait, and Operation Desert Shield became Desert Storm. The U.S. military had crossed a threshold.

The 1970s had opened the door. The 1980s proved women could stand inside it. The 1990s—the Gulf War—would decide whether that door would ever close again.

---

[1] "First Class of Women at West Point," National Museum of the United States Army.
[2] Rachid Haoues, "First Female West Point Graduate Reflects on Historic Anniversary," CBS News, May 28, 2015, https://www.cbsnews.com/news/35-years-since-women-broke-a-military-barrier/
[3] "Susan J. Helms," U.S. Air Force Biography, and "Susan Helms," Encyclopaedia Britannica
[4] "Grace Hopper," American Society of Naval Engineers; and "Admiral Grace Murray Hopper: When Women Were Computers," National WWII Museum
[5] "Army's First Female Deep Sea Diver Reflects on Career During MLK Observance," Defense Visual Information Distribution Service (DVIDS), and Meghann Myers, "First Black Female Deep-Sea Diver Reflects on Her Career," Army Times

Part V— Modern Era: Women on the Frontlines

Chapter 9 — The Gulf War: Women on the Frontlines

"I am a warrior in the time of women warriors; the longing for justice is the sword I carry."

— Sonia Johnson

Kuwait, 1990

WHEN IRAQ'S TANKS ROLLED across the border into Kuwait on an August morning in 1990, the world quickly realized this wasn't just another regional quarrel. It was the first significant test of the post–Cold War order—a high-stakes confrontation driven by oil, power, and shifting alliances.

For years, Iraqi leader Saddam Hussein had been struggling to rebuild his country after a long and costly war with Iran. Deep in debt and desperate for control over more oil, he accused Kuwait of slashing prices and stealing petroleum from shared deposits. Behind the rhetoric was an old territorial claim: Saddam insisted Kuwait had always been part of Iraq. By seizing Kuwait, he could erase debt, dominate oil markets, and expand Iraq's reach across the Persian Gulf.

But the invasion had global consequences. Kuwait's fall placed Saudi Arabia—the world's largest oil supplier—squarely in Saddam's sights. That threat drew a swift and overwhelming response from the United States and a broad, United Nations–backed coalition of nations determined to push Iraq out and uphold the principle that conquest by force would not stand.

Operations Desert Shield and Desert Storm

The front lines of Operation Desert Shield spanned vast stretches of desert and the windswept plains of Kuwait and southern Iraq, with Saudi Arabia serving as the staging ground for coalition forces. The open terrain and brutal heat shaped every decision. Endless supply lines stretched across sand and rock, and survival depended as much on logistics as on military strength.

The buildup began in August 1990, with an enormous defensive effort to protect Saudi Arabia and prepare for a counterattack. When diplomacy failed, Operation Desert Storm began in January 1991.

For weeks, the skies over Iraq echoed with the thunder of precision air strikes aimed at crippling Saddam's command centers, infrastructure, and military forces. Then, in February, the ground war began—and ended almost as quickly as it started. In just 100 hours, coalition troops swept through Iraqi resistance, liberated Kuwait, and brought the conflict to a stunningly swift conclusion.

It was the first major war since Vietnam and the first large-scale conflict of the new era—broadcast live by satellite, guided by computers, and fought with weapons of unprecedented accuracy. The world watched war in real time for the first time.

Women at War: Breaking Old Barriers

When the Gulf War began, women in the U.S. military were still officially barred from direct ground combat roles. Policy allowed them to serve in support—flying planes, tending to the wounded, driving supply trucks, analyzing intelligence, or managing communications—but not in units whose primary mission was to seek out and destroy the enemy.

Yet as the war unfolded, these definitions proved meaningless. The front lines blurred in a war fought across open desert and in the face of missile attacks that reached far beyond any traditional battlefield. Women drove convoys through enemy fire. They operated radar, missile defense systems, and combat aircraft. They served on ships and in command centers where the fighting came to them.

More than 40,000 American women were deployed to the Gulf—the largest number in history up to that time. Hundreds were under attack. Some were wounded. A few were taken prisoner. Their performance under pressure and courage in the face of danger drew widespread attention back home.

A Turning Point for Military Policy

The Gulf War didn't immediately change the rules, but it sparked a national conversation that couldn't be ignored. Congress, in 1991, held hearings to evaluate how women had performed under fire. Two years later, restrictions began to crumble: women could now fly combat aircraft and serve on combat ships. In 1994, the Pentagon issued formal definitions of ground combat roles, narrowing but not eliminating exclusions. It would take another decade, but by 2015, those final barriers had fallen.

Another crucial barrier for women was broken during the Gulf War years: the conflict between being a soldier and a mother at the same time. For most of the 20th century, the women who put on a U.S. military uniform were asked to make a choice that their male counterparts never faced: be a soldier or be a mother—but never both.

Regulations were blunt. During World War II, women in the Women's Army Corps could be discharged if they became pregnant or married a fellow service member. In the decades that followed, policies across all the services treated marriage and motherhood as liabilities for women in uniform, grounds to exclude them from certain roles or to push them out of the force altogether. A woman could serve her country or build a family, but not both at the same time.

By the time of the Gulf War, that hard line had finally begun to crack. Laws and policy changes in the 1970s and 1980s ended automatic discharges for pregnancy, allowing a new generation to raise children while wearing the uniform. This was the first cohort of American servicewomen who could deploy to war knowing they had toddlers at home, teenagers waiting for their calls, or babies they had just kissed goodbye. They were still, on paper, barred from certain combat roles, but they were no longer barred from motherhood itself.

Many of the women who stepped onto planes were both soldiers and mothers, carrying pictures of their kids in their pockets while they shouldered weapons, flew helicopters, drove convoys, and ran field hospitals. When they were wounded, captured, or killed, it was not just as "female soldiers," but as parents whose children would grow up hearing that their mom had gone to war.

Their presence in the desert marked a quiet revolution: for the first time, the United States sent large numbers of women into a major conflict who were also mothers and wives.

Major Rhonda Cornum

Long before anyone called her "the POW doctor," Rhonda Cornum was juggling roles that had nothing to do with headlines or heroism.

She was a scientist and physician, but she was also a mother raising a young daughter through school, sometimes doing it alone while her first marriage strained and eventually ended. For a time, she was a single mom in uniform, trying to balance early-morning formations and late-night studying with the practical, everyday realities of raising a child—finding child care, making it to parent events, and keeping home life steady even when the Army's needs were anything but.

Later, when she married fellow flight surgeon Kory Cornum, the balancing act became even more complex. Now there were two demanding military careers in the same household, plus parenting and marriage to tend to.

During the Gulf War, she was a flight surgeon with the 2-229th Aviation Regiment, a doctor in a helicopter squadron. They were deployed to opposite sides of the theater—Kory in one area, Rhonda flying with an attack helicopter regiment in another—each trusting the other to stay focused, stay alive, and come home to their daughter.

Rhonda's war story begins in the gray light of a chilly Iraqi morning, with hot coffee in her hand and no hint that, within hours, her life would be hanging by a thread. On February 27, 1991, she climbed aboard a Black Hawk that was supposed to fly a routine mission—until the call came in. A U.S. F-16 pilot had been shot down deep inside Iraqi territory. The Black Hawk's orders changed on the spot: it was now a combat search-and-rescue mission into enemy country.[1]

The helicopter raced low over the desert, its crew focused on finding one man in a vast, hostile landscape. The Gulf War's ground campaign was in its final days, yet the battlefield remained deadly. Iraqi forces were alert, armed, and waiting. Somewhere below, anti-aircraft gunners watched the Black Hawk skim across the sky, a dark shape against the fading light. Then their guns opened up. A burst of fire hit the aircraft, and in an instant, the mission shifted from rescue to survival.

Enemy fire tore through the helicopter, sending it into an uncontrollable descent. Inside the cabin, Rhonda had only seconds to brace and hope. The Black Hawk slammed into the desert at high speed, breaking apart in a brutal crash that killed five of the eight soldiers on board. She was one of only three survivors.

When she regained consciousness, she lay amid twisted wreckage, in pain so intense it blurred the edges of the world. Her injuries were severe: both arms were broken, her right knee badly damaged, and a bullet was lodged in her back and shoulder. Shrapnel wounds burned, and the deep ache of broken bones and blood loss throbbed. She was pinned, trapped beneath parts of the helicopter. Even so, she forced herself to think like a doctor, not just a victim. Assess the damage. Breathe. Stay calm. Inch by inch, she dug and wriggled her way out from under the wreckage, dragging her battered body into the open desert. Later, she recalled, her first thoughts were, "Nobody's ever died from pain."

There, she saw the reality of what had happened. The helicopter was shattered. Her crewmates lay dead or badly injured. Help was nowhere in sight. Before she could decide what to do next, armed Iraqi soldiers appeared, weapons raised, encircling the crash site. One grabbed her and pulled her up by her broken arm, sending a fresh wave of agony through her body. At that moment, she understood two things at once: she was still alive—and she was now a prisoner of war.

Rhonda and the other survivors were quickly captured and hustled away from the crash, deeper into Iraqi-controlled territory. The journey into captivity was rough and humiliating. Dragged by her hair, tossed into vehicles, and treated like cargo rather than a human being, her injuries ignored. Along the way, an Iraqi soldier sexually assaulted her, one more violation on a day already filled with pain. Later, she would say that even this assault, as awful as it was, seemed almost small compared to the larger struggle to stay alive, protect others, and endure.

Her captors moved her from place to place—first toward Basra, then on to Baghdad—blindfolded, beaten, and interrogated. The conditions were harsh: cramped cells, limited medical care, and constant uncertainty about what would happen next. In one terrifying episode, she and other prisoners were forced to kneel, surrounded by armed guards, in what felt like a mock execution. Yet even under that pressure, Rhonda held on to a clear sense of purpose. When she was the senior-ranking prisoner, she took responsibility, helping organize and support the others, doing what she could to maintain order and calm amid chaos.

During eight days of captivity, she battled not only physical injury but also the mental strain of being entirely at the enemy's mercy. She could not fix her broken arms or repair her torn knee, but she could control her response. She focused on small signs of hope, such as the moment she realized she could move her fingers again and feel the pain of injured nerves—proof, to her, that her body might heal. She later described that week as "a very bad" one, but insisted it did not define her life. It was something she endured, not something that owned her.

Rhonda Cornum

As the war moved rapidly toward its end and a cease-fire approached, negotiations for the release of prisoners gained momentum. On March 5–6, 1991, Rhonda and other captured Americans were released to the International Committee of the Red Cross and then returned to U.S. forces. She stepped off the plane in a flight suit, arms still injured, but standing on her own—one of only two American women taken prisoner during the Gulf War, and one of the very few people to survive a shootdown, a catastrophic crash, and enemy captivity in the span of a single week.

She did not stop serving when she came home. She stayed in the Army, rose through the ranks to become a brigadier general, and became a powerful voice in the debate over women's roles in combat. Her experience—shot down while on a "non-combat" mission, wounded, captured, and still taking charge as a leader—exposed how artificial those old rules really were.

Her story helped push the military toward recognizing that women were already facing combat conditions and deserved both the opportunity and the acknowledgment that came with that reality.

In the years after her capture and release, Rhonda made a deliberate choice about how to tell her story. She refused to let eight days in Iraqi hands become the center of her identity. When she spoke publicly, she framed the shootdown and captivity as a brutal but contained chapter inside a much bigger book—one that included a long medical career, senior command roles, marriage, motherhood, and even raising horses on a farm. She did not deny the trauma, but she refused to be reduced to it.

To her, resilience meant that her life was defined not by the worst week she ever lived, but by everything she built before and after—doctor, officer, wife, and mom, all at once. Her story is not just about a crash or captivity; it is about a mindset. Faced with broken bones, blood loss, assault, fear, and loss, she chose to see herself not as a victim but as a survivor and a leader. The helicopter went down. Her body was battered. But her will—to-live, to lead, to return to duty, never broke.

Melissa Rathbun-Nealy

When Melissa Rathbun-Nealy went to war, she was a 20-year-old newlywed and Army truck driver responsible for moving vehicles and supplies near the front. It was all fairly routine until the night her jeep crossed into Iraqi territory, and she became the first U.S. woman officially listed as Missing in Action since World War II.

On a dark January night in 1991, a battered Army jeep rattled across the flat desert near the Saudi–Kuwaiti border, carrying a young truck driver who had never expected to make history. Specialist Melissa Rathbun-Nealy, a young soldier from Michigan, was part of the 233rd Transportation Company. Her job was dangerous but straightforward: move supplies and vehicles through a war zone that was anything but orderly.

Somewhere in that maze of night, sand, and confusion, she and fellow soldier Specialist David Lockett crossed from relative safety into enemy territory. They did not know it at first. The desert can be deceiving: the same low scrub, the same hard-packed earth. But soon the signs became clear. Strange tracks. Unfamiliar shapes in the distance. Then the headlights. Iraqi forces appeared out of the darkness, and in an instant, Melissa's role changed from driver to captive.

Their vehicles were hit by Iraqi fire, and both Melissa and David were wounded: she had a bullet wound through her upper arm and shrapnel in her lower arm; he was also injured. Their jeep was stopped, and weapons were leveled at them. The two Americans were pulled from the vehicle. In those tense moments, the Iraqis considered leaving David behind, but Melissa refused to abandon him. Her insistence that he be taken with her meant both soldiers went into captivity together.[2]

Back at home, the Army could not reach them by radio. The jeep was found with blood in the cab and no sign of its crew. For days, officials could say only that the two were missing. Melissa became the only U.S. woman listed as Missing in Action in the Gulf War, and the first U.S. servicewoman officially reported MIA since World War II.

Newspapers picked up her story. Her name appeared in headlines and television reports, sometimes simply as "the missing woman soldier in the Gulf." For many Americans, the idea that a young female truck driver might be lost behind enemy lines—and possibly in Iraqi hands—was chilling and new.

Inside Iraq, Melissa and David were moved north to Basra, a key command city already under heavy Allied bombing. There, they were held under guard, often in isolation, with little information and no control over what would happen next. She later recalled being alone much of the time, unsure whether anyone even knew she was alive. Her world shrank to the size of a cell and the sound of distant explosions.

For more than a month, Melissa remained a prisoner of war. Her parents in Michigan pleaded for her safety, even addressing Saddam Hussein directly in hopes of mercy. In early March 1991, as cease-fire talks took hold and prisoner exchanges began, the waiting finally ended.

Melissa Rathbun-Nealy and David Lockett were among the first groups of American POWs released by Iraq, part of a ten-person group turned over to the Red Cross and then to U.S. officials. Cameras captured her smiling shyly, surprised to learn that her face had been on magazine covers in Europe and on front pages across the United States. She had gone into the war as a little-known transportation specialist; she came out as the first American woman POW of the Persian Gulf War and the first U.S. woman officially listed MIA in a conflict since the 1940s.

In the weeks that followed, offers poured in—interviews, book deals, public appearances. Melissa pushed back against the narrative that she was either a helpless victim or a flawless hero. She insisted she was a soldier who did her job, was captured, survived, and came home. After recovering, she returned to duty, later serving as a heavy equipment operator and continuing her Army career.

Her capture forced the country to confront the reality that women were no longer just "near" the front lines—they were on them, driving into danger, getting lost, getting captured, and facing the same risks as their male peers. Her calm, matter-of-fact telling of her story helped shift the perception that she was not a symbol of weakness but proof that women could endure the harshest tests of war and still stand tall when they came home.

In the years after her release, Melissa's life shifted from the sand and smoke of the Gulf back to something more familiar—a wife, mother, and veteran living with chronic health problems that doctors linked to her service. She had daughters, and the woman once known only as "America's first female POW in the Gulf" found herself packing school lunches, helping with homework, and sitting in tiny chairs at school events, telling her story to her children's classmates so they could understand what war really meant.

The balancing act was constant: managing fatigue and lingering medical issues, carrying the weight of memories she did not always want to revisit, yet choosing, again and again, to show up fully as a mom—present, patient, and honest—while also honoring the soldier she had been.

Melissa Rathbun-Nealy

Lieutenant Phoebe Jeter

Lieutenant Phoebe Jeter watched the radar screen bloom with danger before anyone outside her van knew what was coming. Somewhere in the dark, Iraqi launch crews had fired SCUD missiles into the night sky, crude but deadly weapons capable of carrying conventional or even chemical warheads. Ahead of her, the electronic traces of those missiles bent into shallow arcs—headed straight toward her sector, toward her own soldiers and the units they were protecting. As an air defense artillery officer leading a Patriot missile control team, Phoebe knew there were only seconds to act. She had trained for years for this moment. Now it was here.

Her platoon was all male, a fact that drew attention only because of what happened next. Calm under pressure, Jeter called out the tracks, confirmed what she saw on the screen, and began issuing orders. Fire missions rolled off her tongue in a steady, practiced rhythm as she ordered her crew to launch Patriot missiles against the incoming SCUDs. Tube after tube flared, sending interceptors screaming skyward to meet the threat. In that brief window, there was no room for doubt or hesitation. If she misjudged the data before her, those SCUDs could slam into the very base where she and her men stood.

The Patriots found their marks. High above the desert, the missiles intersected, and at least two Iraqi SCUDs were destroyed before they could reach their targets. On the ground, soldiers watched the sky erupt in bright bursts of light, unaware that the calm voice behind the intercept belonged to a young Black woman from South Carolina.[3]

In official Army history, that engagement would later be written up as the work of "the first female Scudbuster," a lieutenant who led a fifteen-man Patriot control team and successfully engaged enemy missiles in combat. For Phoebe, it was not about being first. It was about doing her job—reading the screen, trusting her training, and protecting her people.

Her story rippled outward after the war, especially in accounts of Black women's service in the Gulf. Advocates pointed to her performance as a clear example of how women were already operating at the heart of modern combat, even when the rules still pretended otherwise.

She was not in an infantry trench or a tank, but the decisions she made under pressure meant the difference between life and death, just as surely as any firefight on the ground. In that cramped control van, with alarms sounding and data streaming in, Lieutenant Phoebe Jeter helped prove that women could stand at the very center of the battlefield—quietly guiding the weapons that shielded everyone else.

Phoebe Jeter

The Gulf War was another turning point for military women. It began with the first generation of women who had finally won the right to serve and to be mothers, yet were still officially excluded from "direct combat." On paper, they were still considered support. In reality, they were flying into missile fire, driving through ambush zones, hunting SCUDs, and surviving capture and torture.

Their stories—Rhonda Cornum's broken body and unbroken will, Melissa Rathbun-Nealy's weeks as a missing POW, and Phoebe Jeter's calm voice guiding Patriot missiles—make it impossible to pretend that women were anything but at the heart of the fight.

By the time the shooting stopped in 1991, the policy fiction had been exposed. The rules still claimed women were shielded from the most dangerous roles, but the desert had shown something very different: women bleeding, leading, commanding, and coming home with the same scars as their male peers. This generation forced Congress, the Pentagon, and the public to confront a simple truth—combat was no longer a clear line on a map, and women were already crossing it.

The women who went to war after 9/11 inherited a battlefield and a bureaucracy reshaped by the Gulf War pioneers. In the War on Terror, women would deploy not as rare exceptions but in huge numbers, serve in ground units that lived under constant attack, and eventually see the final legal barriers to combat lifted. The quiet revolution that started in the sands of Kuwait and Iraq would become explicit policy: women not just near the fight, or accidentally in it, but fully, officially part of it.

[1] Rhonda Cornum, "Crew Endurance: A New Perspective," United States Army Aviation Digest 35 (November–December 1989).
[2] "Female POWs Recall Iraqi Captivity During Persian Gulf War," Los Angeles Times, February 14, 1991.
[3] "Women and the Persian Gulf War," American Aviation Women's Association.

Chapter 10 — Women and the War on Terror

"Never forget."

ON A BRIGHT, ORDINARY Tuesday morning in September 2001, the sky over the East Coast was so clear it seemed almost unreal—deep blue, calm, harmless. Then, in the span of a few minutes, passenger jets became weapons. One after another, four hijacked planes veered off course and slammed into American landmarks: two into the twin towers of the World Trade Center in New York City, one into the Pentagon just outside Washington, D.C., and one into a quiet field in Pennsylvania after passengers chose to fight back rather than let the hijackers reach their target.

People across the country stood frozen in front of televisions, watching skyscrapers burn and then collapse live on the morning news. Nearly 3,000 lives were lost in a single day, and with them went something Americans had taken for granted—that oceans and distance somehow shielded the United States from large-scale attacks.

In the stunned days that followed, President George W. Bush and Congress gave this moment a name and a response. They declared a new kind of war, not against a single nation with borders and uniforms, but against a loose, shadowy network of terrorists—beginning with al-Qaeda and the Taliban government in Afghanistan that had sheltered and trained them.

The "War on Terror" was the name the United States gave to the resulting long, global campaign against terrorism that began after those attacks and stretched across decades and continents. It was not one single war, but a series of linked conflicts, military operations, and security measures aimed first at al-Qaeda, then at other extremist groups that grew and morphed over time. For the generation that fought it, this wasn't a brief desert campaign with clear start and end dates; it was the backdrop of their entire adult lives.

Afghanistan

The first major battlefield of this war was Afghanistan. When the Taliban refused to hand over Osama bin Laden and al-Qaeda leaders, the U.S. and its allies launched airstrikes and then ground operations in October 2001 under the banner "Operation Enduring Freedom." The early goal was clear and narrow: topple the Taliban, destroy al-Qaeda training camps, and prevent Afghanistan from being used as a base for more attacks.

The Taliban government fell quickly, but a stubborn insurgency grew, and what began as a targeted operation turned into a long counterinsurgency and nation-building effort that lasted, in different forms, until the final U.S. withdrawal from Afghanistan in 2021.

Iraq

In 2003, the War on Terror widened dramatically with the U.S.-led invasion of Iraq. The Bush administration argued that Saddam Hussein's regime might be developing weapons of mass destruction and claimed Iraq was part of the broader terrorist threat, even though direct ties to the

9/11 attacks were never proven. The Iraqi government collapsed quickly, but the aftermath—insurgency, sectarian violence, and the later rise of the Islamic State (ISIS)—turned Iraq into another grinding, open-ended front in the same global campaign.

Over time, the War on Terror spread beyond these two main wars. U.S. forces, intelligence agencies, and partners carried out operations and drone strikes against terrorist groups in places like Pakistan, Yemen, Somalia, and Syria.

At home, new laws and agencies—such as the Department of Homeland Security—reshaped airport security, surveillance, immigration, and emergency planning, all justified as part of preventing another 9/11. What began as a response to a single day of horror slowly became a permanent security posture that touched everyday life.

For the women who served in uniform during this era, the War on Terror meant repeated deployments, a battlefield with no fixed front lines, and enemies who used roadside bombs and suicide attacks instead of tanks and uniformed armies. They patrolled dusty streets, rode in convoys that could be hit at any moment, flew close-air support over firefights, and staffed intelligence and special operations units tracking terrorist networks.

As the years went on, their constant presence under fire helped push the military to finally drop the last legal bans on women in ground combat, turning the quiet reality of the Gulf War into explicit policy.

Nada Bakos

Nada Bakos did not hunt terrorists with a rifle or a rifle squad. She hunted them with questions, patterns, and maps spread across a conference table under fluorescent light.

As a CIA analyst after 9/11, she stepped into a world where the battlefield looked less like a trench and more like a maze of phone numbers, safe houses, bank transfers, and whispered names. Her job was to make sense of that maze, to turn fragments of information into a picture clear enough for others to act on. At the center of that picture, for years, stood one man: Abu Musab al-Zarqawi, a Jordanian extremist who would build al-Qaeda in Iraq, the group that later evolved into the Islamic State.

Nada became one of the agency's lead "targeters"—the person whose work connects raw intelligence to a real human being on the ground. She and her team sifted through reports, intercepted communications, interrogation summaries, and tips from allies, searching for anything that could reveal where Zarqawi was, whom he trusted, and how he moved.

It was painstaking work: every detail had to be verified, every assumption challenged. One wrong conclusion could mean striking the wrong house, missing the right convoy, or letting a key opportunity slip away. But each small piece—a license plate here, a new courier there—slowly tightened the circle around him.

Her role wasn't just technical; it was also political. As Zarqawi's attacks tore through Iraq—suicide bombings, beheadings, and strikes aimed at sparking sectarian war—

Nada and other analysts had to brief senior leaders and push for the operations they believed were needed. That meant walking into high-level meetings, sometimes challenging policymakers' views of the threat, and arguing for a targeting picture grounded in her team's work. In her memoir, *The Targeter*, she describes the tension of those years: wanting to move fast enough to stop the next attack, but carefully enough to avoid deadly mistakes, all while navigating the pressures and doubts coming from above.[1]

In June 2006, the work paid off. After years of chasing leads, the U.S. finally located Zarqawi at a safe house outside Baqubah in Iraq. Acting on the intelligence picture that analysts like Nada had assembled, American aircraft struck the compound, killing Zarqawi and several associates. For the public, it was a headline: the death of a brutal terror leader. For Nada, it was proof that quiet, unseen labor in windowless rooms could change the course of a war.

The organization Zarqawi built would not disappear, but its most volatile and charismatic leader was gone because one woman had followed the trail all the way to a specific roof in a particular village.

Looking back, Nada has framed her story as more than a personal victory. She uses it to show what modern intelligence work really looks like—and to push back against the idea that women in national security are somehow secondary or supporting players.

In reality, she was central to one of the most critical manhunts of the early War on Terror, shaping decisions that would echo through Iraq and beyond. Her life as "the targeter" shows another side of war: not just the soldiers on patrol, but the analysts whose quiet persistence turns information into action, and whose choices can bring some of the world's most dangerous men within reach.

Sgt. Monica Lin Brown

The blast hit first—a thunderous crack that swallowed everything else and threw dirt, smoke, and metal into the Afghan air.

A convoy of American soldiers had been moving along a rough, rutted road in Paktia Province when an improvised explosive device detonated under one of the vehicles, ripping it open and leaving soldiers scattered, bleeding, and dazed on the ground. Small-arms fire followed from nearby positions, rounds snapping over the heads of anyone who tried to move.

In the middle of that chaos, a 19-year-old Latina Army medic, Sgt. Monica Lin Brown, heard the call every medic dreads and trains for: "We've got wounded!"

She did not stay behind cover. Monica grabbed her aid bag and ran toward the smoking vehicle, sprinting across open ground that was still under enemy fire. The road offered almost no protection. Bullets cracked around her as she reached the wounded soldiers and dropped to her knees beside them.

One was badly hurt, bleeding heavily. Another was drifting in and out of consciousness. Monica forced herself to focus on the basics—airway, bleeding, breathing—blocking out the noise, the fear, and the knowledge that she could be hit at any second.

Realizing the damaged vehicle could still be targeted or catch fire, she helped drag the wounded to a shallow ditch nearby—the only cover available. In that narrow strip of dirt, with rounds still coming in, she worked quickly: applying tourniquets and bandages, administering IVs, talking to the injured men to keep them awake, and reassuring them that help was on the way. The ditch became an improvised aid station, and Monica refused to leave until every one of her patients was stabilized and ready for evacuation.

Her actions that day saved lives. They also shattered the idea, still enshrined in policy at the time, that women were somehow not "really" in combat. Monica was a medic assigned to a support role, but the battlefield in Afghanistan did not care about job titles. She did precisely what any frontline soldier is expected to do under fire: move toward danger, protect others, and keep fighting—in her case, fighting to keep hearts beating and lungs working.

For those actions, Monica Lin Brown was awarded the Silver Star, one of the nation's highest awards for valor in combat.[2] When the medal was pinned to her uniform, she became only the second woman since World War II to receive the Silver Star for bravery in direct combat.

The image of a young Latina woman, honored for running through gunfire to save her fellow soldiers, became a landmark moment in the public story of women in war—a clear, undeniable scene that showed what had already been true on the ground for years: women were not just present in the War on Terror; they were among its most courageous fighters.

Monica Lin Brown

Lori Ann Piestewa and Shoshana Johnson

They rolled into Iraq together in the same unit, two young women in the 507th Maintenance Company, doing what the Army had trained them to do: keep the war moving.

Specialist Lori Ann Piestewa, a Hopi soldier from Arizona, drove heavy vehicles and looked after the soldiers around her with the same steady care she showed her own two children back home. Specialist Shoshana Johnson, a Black single mother born in Panama and raised in Texas, worked as a cook, feeding troops in a war that was just beginning.

Neither woman wore an infantry badge. On paper, they were support. On the roads outside Nasiriyah in March 2003, there was no such thing as "support" and "combat." There was only the ambush.

The 507th was pushing forward in a long convoy when things went wrong—wrong turns, bad maps, and suddenly they were alone in hostile territory. Iraqi forces opened fire from the sides of the road and from buildings along the route. Vehicles stalled, crashed, or were hit. In that chaos, Lori fought to keep control of her truck, slammed into a jackknifed tractor-trailer, and took fire as the ambush closed around them. She was gravely wounded and would not survive her injuries.[3]

At 23, Lori became the first woman killed in the Iraq War and the first Native American woman in U.S. history to die in combat. Her loss was felt not only by her unit but across Indian Country, where flags were lowered, and prayers rose for a daughter, mother, and warrior.

For Shoshana Johnson, the same attack turned into a different kind of ordeal. When her vehicle was disabled and surrounded, she was shot in both ankles, unable to run, bleeding, and in pain. Iraqi fighters dragged her and several others from the wreckage, weapons pointed at them, and marched them away as prisoners.

Within days, footage of Johnson and other captured soldiers appeared on Iraqi television and then on screens around the world: the first Black female American POW, sitting rigid in a metal chair, face tight with pain and fear, answering questions through an interpreter.

Shoshana Johnson

At home, her parents watched their daughter's image in shock, and the country realized, again, that women and men of color were on the line in this war just like everyone else.

For weeks, Shoshana endured captivity—makeshift cells, rough interrogations, and little medical care for her wounds. She did not know if she would ever see her daughter again. Then, in early April, U.S. Marines sweeping through the area around Nasiriyah burst into the building where she and other POWs were held and freed them.

Cameras captured her being carried to safety, her ankles still bandaged. Her return, alongside other rescued prisoners, became a national story, a living reminder of the price paid by those who did not choose the firefight but found themselves in it anyway.

Lori Ann Piestewa
http://www.army.mil/-images/2007/11/01/9851/

Their lives and losses show that by the early 2000s, women were changing forever what a "typical" American soldier looked like.

Women in Special Operations

They were never supposed to be on the front lines—at least not on paper. Yet, starting around 2010, a new group of women quietly moved into the heart of America's most secretive missions. They were called Cultural Support Teams, or CSTs, small handpicked units of female soldiers who would live, work, and patrol alongside Special Operations forces in Afghanistan and Iraq.

Their presence began with a simple problem that no high-tech weapon could solve: in many conservative villages, male soldiers could not speak to, search, or even look directly at local women without causing offense or shutting down cooperation.

The legal and policy changes that opened this door had been building for years. By 2010, women were still officially barred from specific ground combat jobs. Yet previous reforms had already allowed them into more and more operational roles—intelligence, military police, civil affairs, aviation, and special operations support.

A formal order that year authorized commanders to draw on this pool of experienced female soldiers and attach them to elite units such as the Army Rangers, Green Berets, and other Special Operations teams. It was a workaround within the existing rules: the women were not technically "in" the special operations unit, but they went wherever the unit went.

On the ground, the mission was both simple and incredibly delicate. When a Special Operations team hit a compound at night or visited a village during the day, the CST members moved in behind or alongside them, peeling off to gather the half of the population the men could not reach. They searched women at checkpoints, spoke with mothers and daughters in courtyards and back rooms, asked what they had seen, and listened for details that might reveal hidden weapons, bomb-makers, or insurgent safe houses. In many homes, they were the first American soldiers the local women had ever been able to look in the eye.

Trust was their main weapon. While the men cleared rooms and secured perimeters, CST members sat on floors, accepted tea, admired babies, and asked quiet, careful questions. They listened to complaints about checkpoints, prices, and security, and explained why the soldiers kept returning to this village or that road. In return, Afghan and Iraqi women sometimes shared things they would never tell a man: which strangers had appeared in the area, where new men were sleeping, who had suddenly come into money, and whose son had started disappearing at night. Piece by piece, those conversations became intelligence.

The work was dangerous. CST soldiers wore body armor, carried rifles, and walked the same dusty paths and narrow alleys as the men they supported. They rode in helicopters and armored trucks that improvised explosive devices could hit, and they entered compounds not knowing who or what was on the other side of the door. Yet their official status remained "attached," not assigned to combat units—a legal distinction that lagged far behind reality. Their performance, however, spoke louder than paperwork. Commanders began to request CSTs by name, describing them as critical to mission success when operating among local families.

In the larger story of women in the War on Terror, these teams mark a significant shift. Earlier generations had to prove that women could endure combat when war came to them anyway; CSTs were created because commanders now understood that women brought capabilities men could not offer in these cultures. Their success became part of the evidence policymakers cited when the U.S. finally lifted the last formal bans on women in ground combat roles between 2013 and 2015.

By then, the women of the Cultural Support Teams had already been doing that work in the shadows for years—quietly opening doors, earning trust, and helping win a different kind of ground in a very different type of war.

Legacy and Impact

The War on Terror finally closed the gap between what the military said women could do and what women were already doing.

By Afghanistan and Iraq, the fiction of the "rear area" was gone. Convoys were ambushed. Bases were shelled. Medics, intelligence specialists, pilots, military police, and support troops were in constant contact with the enemy. Women were wounded, captured, decorated for valor, and killed in action—not as anomalies, but as a matter of course.

By the end of the War on Terror, women like the ones in this chapter were no longer exceptions; they were the pattern. They had flown attack helicopters over Iraq, patrolled Afghan valleys, kicked down doors with special operations teams, and sifted through streams of data to find the men who planned bombings from the shadows. They were shot at, blown up, taken prisoner, and promoted. Their names and "firsts" trace the slow, uneven way policy finally caught up with reality.

Tammy Duckworth's Black Hawk went down over Iraq in 2004 when an RPG tore through the cockpit, costing her both legs and nearly her life. She came home in a wheelchair and chose more service: first at VA, then in Congress, and finally in the U.S. Senate, turning her own wounds into a public fight for veterans and military families.

Capt. Vernice "FlyGirl" Armour flew attack helicopters for the Marine Corps in the 2003 invasion and became known as the first African American female combat pilot in Marine aviation, a living rebuke to the old idea that cockpits and combat were for men only.[4]

In the Marine Corps—the last service to open many doors—loss and breakthrough sat side by side. Maj. Megan McClung, a former Naval Academy trailblazer, was killed in Iraq in 2006 and is remembered as the first female Marine officer to die there, a reminder that women were sharing the highest costs of the war. A decade later, 1st Lt. Marina Hierl became the first woman to graduate the Marine Corps Infantry Officer Course, earning the right to lead an infantry platoon in the very kind of ground units that had long been closed to women.[5]

Some of the most important work stayed almost invisible.

Senior Chief Shannon Kent, a Navy cryptologic warfare specialist, deployed multiple times to Iraq and worked alongside special operations forces, using language skills and signals intelligence to hunt insurgent networks before being killed in Syria in 2019.[6]

In the Army, Capt. Kristen Griest and 1st Lt. Shaye Haver pushed through one of the toughest courses the service offers, becoming the first women to graduate Ranger School and setting the stage for women to serve in elite light infantry units that had once been entirely male.[7]

Major General Angela Salinas

At the senior level, leaders like Maj. Gen. Angela Salinas showed where this path could lead. She rose from enlisted Marine to become the first Hispanic woman promoted to general in the Corps, eventually commanding a major recruiting force that shaped future generations of Marines. Her career underscored a simple truth: when women are allowed to serve, they do not just fill slots—they change the institution.

The young women who went to Iraq and Afghanistan flew, fought, led, bled, and then kept serving—as officers, lawmakers, generals, and mentors. Their "firsts" will one day read like a list of obvious jobs, but in this era they were proof that women warriors were no longer the exception. They were the new normal.

---

[1] Anne Cantrell, "On Target," MSU News, October 15, 2013
[2] SPC Micah Clare, "2nd Woman Since WWII Gets Silver Star," United States Army.
[3] Osha Gray Davidson, "A Wrong Turn in the Desert," Rolling Stone, May 27, 2004.
[4] "Vernice Armour, Captain, U.S. Marine Corps," Foundation for Women Warriors.
[5] "For the First Time in Marine Corps History, a Woman Is in Charge of an Infantry Platoon," CNN, August 10, 2018.
[6] "Shannon M. Kent," Military Times, Honoring the Fallen.
[7] "Two Women Graduate from Army Ranger School," CNN, August 21, 2015,

Conclusion

If there is one lesson that repeats across every chapter of this book, it is that war does not care what policy says.

On paper, women were always supposed to stand just outside the blast radius—nurses but not fighters, drivers but not warriors, "support" but never the tip of the spear. In practice, from the women in the backcountry of a new nation, to volunteers of World Wars to the women threading their way through SCUD fire in the Gulf, the line between "noncombat" and combat has always dissolved the moment real danger appeared.

Across the decades, the armed forces tried again and again to draw boundaries around women's service: certain jobs were "appropriate," others forbidden; leadership was acceptable in some spaces but not in the ones that most clearly defined war. Those lines held only until the mission pressed too hard. When the country needed codebreakers, women cracked enemy ciphers. When it needed pilots, they flew. When convoys turned deadly in Iraq or medevac flights were shot down over the desert, women like Lori Piestewa and Monica Brown did the work in front of them, whether or not the rulebook gave them permission.

Intelligence fused into operations, turning analysts like Nada Bakos into central actors in manhunts. Supply runs, like those of the 507th, became ambush magnets. Bases that looked "safe" on a map became targets for rockets and complex attacks. Women learned the hard way that "support" was just another word for life-and-death work. By the time combat exclusions were finally lifted, the argument had already been settled in scars, Silver Stars, prosthetic limbs, and casualty notifications.

This is also where we reflect on what it meant to *fully* serve.

Every woman in these pages carried more than one identity: daughters and mothers, wives and partners, tribal citizens and immigrants, voters, professionals, and neighbors—who also happened to be soldiers, pilots, analysts, cryptologists, and special operations enablers.

Some, like Tammy Duckworth, became public symbols. Others—CST members moving through Afghan courtyards, Marines cracking old barriers—were used heavily and praised quietly, if at all.

Yet the record, once you look closely, is clear: women's labor made these wars function. They moved fuel and food, interrogated detainees, built the intelligence picture, stabilized the wounded in ditches and tents, commanded teams of volunteers or troops, and held the fragile human center of unit life together far from home.

The final truth is simple and uncomfortable: institutions tend to change only after individuals have already paid the price of doing the job under outdated rules. The women in these chapters lived and served in that gap—between what was officially permitted and what the mission actually required. They fought in the blind spots of policy, in the "gray areas" history likes to smooth over, in the spaces where the paperwork said they were not really there.

Mothers, Sisters, Soldiers, Spies closes that gap on purpose. It is not a victory lap or a simple celebration. It is a correction: an attempt to put women back into the frame of the wars they helped fight and sustain. Because if a nation is willing to ask for someone's service—ask her to fly, to bleed, to endure captivity, to come home changed—it owes her, at minimum, the truth about who served, how they served, and what they actually did.

Acknowledgements

This book rests on records—official, personal, and imperfect—and on the people who preserved them.

I am indebted first to the women whose service anchors these pages. Many served under policies that failed to name what they were doing or to recognize the risks they carried. Their records survive because they showed up, did the work, and left a trace strong enough to be found later.

I am grateful to archivists, historians, and librarians who made verification possible, particularly those who steward military collections, oral histories, and government records. The work of the Library of Congress Veterans History Project, service-branch historical offices, and independent scholars ensures that individual service does not dissolve into statistics.

This book also owes a debt to journalists and contemporaneous reporters who documented these wars as they unfolded. Their dispatches, interviews, and investigations often captured truths long before policy or official histories caught up.

Thank you to the veterans and families who shared testimony, correspondence, and context—sometimes decades after events that were never meant to be remembered publicly. Your willingness to preserve detail matters more than you may know.

Finally, this work was shaped by the conviction that accuracy is not optional. Historical clarity requires restraint, verification, and the discipline to say "we do not know" when the record does not support a claim. Any errors that remain are mine alone.

This book exists because memory was kept, even when recognition was not.

My appreciation also extends to the early readers and researchers who offered thoughtful feedback, identified errors, and helped refine the narrative so that it remained both accurate and accessible.

Finally, I am grateful to those who encouraged this project from its earliest concept through its final pages. Your support, questions, and insistence on truth over myth sustained the work at every stage.

Notes on Sources

This book is a work of narrative history written for general readers. It draws on a wide range of historical materials to present accurate, verifiable accounts of women whose wartime labor has often been overlooked, minimized, or misclassified in the official record.

Research for this book combines contemporary documents—such as letters, diaries, service records, pension files, newspapers, photographs, and government reports—with the work of established historians, museums, and archival institutions. In the twentieth century and later, declassified records and formal investigations were used where available. When firsthand documentation is limited or silent, the book relies on well-regarded scholarly studies that clearly identify their evidence.

Women's wartime history presents particular challenges not because women were absent, but because their work was frequently labeled as informal, auxiliary, or voluntary—even when it involved sustained risk, specialized skill, and institutional dependence. As a result, women often appear in historical records indirectly, through administrative disputes, court cases, benefit claims, or commentary written by others. Absence from the record should not be mistaken for absence from events.

To address these gaps, this book places individual lives within their institutional context: laws, policies, unit structures, occupational classifications, and postwar benefit systems. These frameworks help clarify what women were permitted to do, what they were barred from doing, and how those boundaries shifted under pressure.

All factual claims are documented in endnotes for readers who wish to explore the sources further, while the main text remains focused on narrative clarity and historical context.

Espionage and contested narratives

Intelligence work presents additional challenges. Espionage is designed to leave limited documentation, and secrecy has encouraged exaggeration and mythmaking—particularly in stories involving women. Where accounts are disputed, this book favors corroborated evidence and clearly distinguishes between documented facts, contemporary beliefs, and later interpretations.

When evidence is uncertain, the text clearly signals that uncertainty, and the endnotes explain why. Dramatic stories are not treated as proof simply because they are popular.

Race, class, and unequal visibility

Race and class profoundly shaped who could serve, how women were assigned, and whether their service was recorded or rewarded. Segregation restricted roles and promotion for many women of color, while Indigenous women's experiences often survive only through records created by federal authorities or outside observers. Working-class women's labor—especially in industry and informal wartime roles—appears unevenly across local and national archives.

Rather than isolating these histories, the book integrates race and class as forces that shaped women's wartime experiences in every period. Where evidence is fragmentary, the book avoids speculation and instead reconstructs the most accurate picture possible from multiple sources.

Numbers and claims

When this book uses numbers—such as enlistment totals, staffing levels, casualty figures, or policy dates—they come from government records or well-established historical studies. In cases where sources differ, the text reflects those differences rather than forcing false precision.

The purpose of this research is simple: accuracy. Women's wartime history does not require embellishment to be compelling. The documented record—of work performed, risks accepted, limits imposed, and recognition delayed—is powerful on its own. Notes are included for readers who wish to explore the sources further, but the focus of the book remains on telling these stories clearly, responsibly, and without distortion.

Authors Note

This book was written against a familiar problem: women appear everywhere in war records, yet rarely at the center of the story.

The decision to write Mothers, Sisters, Soldiers, Spies was not driven by the absence of women from military history, but by how often their service is misclassified, minimized, or explained away. Women are frequently described as "supporting" wars they were, in fact, helping to run. The record does not sustain that distinction.

This book also resists the urge to smooth history into inevitability. The policy changes that now appear obvious were contested, delayed, and often resisted. Many of the women in these pages served before institutions were prepared to acknowledge what they were doing. They carried the burden of that mismatch—between permission and necessity—personally.

I have chosen verifiability over completeness. Every individual profiled here can be tied to documented service. There are many more stories that deserve to be told, and their absence should not be mistaken for insignificance. It reflects the limits of the surviving record, not the limits of women's participation.

Finally, this book is not an argument about what should have happened. It is an account of what did happen. War is unsentimental. It uses the people available to it. The women in these pages were used, relied upon, and, in many cases, tested beyond what the language of the policy allowed at the time.

If this book corrects anything, it is not history's outcome, but its framing. The women were there. The record proves it.

About the Author

Maureen Safford has spent more than 25 years as a writer working in storytelling and public understanding. Across that career, one principle has remained constant: stories shape what people remember—and what they overlook.

A lifelong student of history, she is particularly drawn to the moments where official narratives fail to capture lived reality. Her work focuses on uncovering how history actually functioned on the ground, especially in places where women's roles were essential, constrained, or deliberately minimized.

Her approach to narrative storytelling by treating historical subjects not as abstractions or symbols, but as individuals.

A Request from the Author

If this book spoke to you or provided helpful context on the lives of women throughout America's military history, a short book review is appreciated.

Reviews keep nonfiction history accessible to future generations and are greatly appreciated by authors and independent publishers like us.

The full catalog of books by Marueen Safford and Unbound Press can be found at

www.unboundpressbooks.com

Preview of Women on the Prairie, by Ward McLendon and Unbound Press Books

The following pages include a preview from Women on the Prairie available at bookstores and online at Amazon.com, Barnes and Noble, and www.unboundpressbooks.com

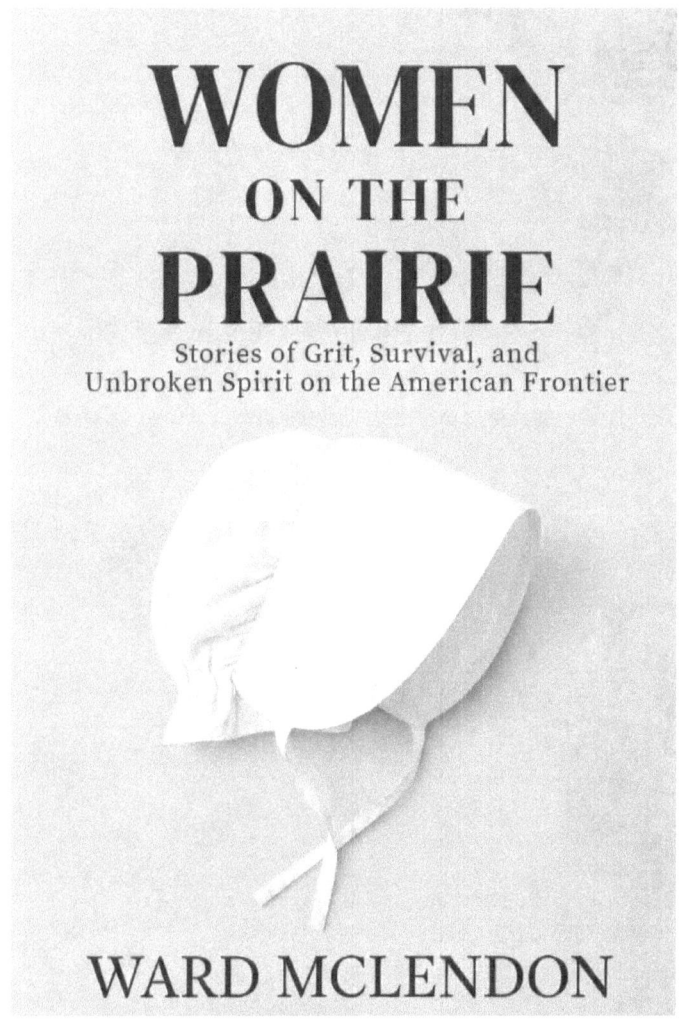

Chapter 1: Across the Overland Trails: Women and the Great Western Migration

"Courage, my daughters. The West is yet unwon."

—Abigail Scott Duniway

Westward Bound

The land stretched endlessly before her, a sea of prairie grass rippling in the wind like waves on an ocean. Sarah Mitchell stood at the edge of what would become her family's claim—160 acres of possibility and hardship rolled into one. It was 1873, and like thousands of other women, she had just arrived in Nebraska Territory with nothing but a wagon full of belongings, a husband with dreams bigger than his experience, and a determination that would prove more valuable than either.

Sarah was just one of more than 400,000 emigrants who crossed the plains and mountains of North America in one of the largest overland migrations in world history. The Oregon Trail, California Trail, and Mormon Trail spanned thousands of miles, connecting the settled East with the uncertain promise of the West. While men often dominate the popular image of this great migration—driving oxen, scouting ahead, or negotiating with other travelers—women were just as present and vital. Their work, journals, endurance, and emotional labor made the journey possible.

We will explore what the westward trek meant for those women: the physical exhaustion, the emotional strain, the domestic burdens carried across continents, the relationships forged and tested on the trail, and the encounters with Native peoples whose homelands the emigrants crossed.

More than anything, we will examine how the trail transformed women, turning many from sheltered residents of eastern towns and farms into adaptable, resilient pioneers able to survive the harshest environments.

A Journey Few Women Were Prepared For

Most women who stepped onto the Overland Trail had never traveled more than a few miles from home. They had grown up in settled communities: small New England towns with white church steeples, Ohio farmsteads bordered by split-rail fences, and Missouri river settlements crowded with mills and trading posts. Life in these communities followed a familiar rhythm shaped by seasons, neighbors, and predictable routines.

Westward migration was almost never a choice initiated by women. It was usually a decision made by husbands, fathers, or extended families driven by economic pressure, crop failures, rising land prices in the East, or the promise of cheap, fertile acreage waiting beyond the Missouri River. Others were lured by gold in California, religious freedom in Utah, or the belief, fueled by newspapers and land agents, that a family's entire fortune could be remade on the far side of the continent.

To read more, find Women on the Prairie on Amazon, Barnes and Noble or www.unboundpressbooks.com

www.ingramcontent.com/pod-product-compliance
Lightning Source LLC
LaVergne TN
LVHW040135080526
838202LV00042B/2909